INDIA-INDONESIA RELATIONS
A CIVILISATIONAL PARTNERSHIP

INDIA-INDONESIA RELATIONS
A CIVILISATIONAL PARTNERSHIP

Edited by

VINOD ANAND

Vivekananda International Foundation

PENTAGON PRESS LLP

First published in 2025 by
PENTAGON PRESS LLP
206, Peacock Lane, Shahpur Jat
New Delhi-110049, India
Contact: 011-26490600

Typeset in Adobe Garamond, 11.5 Point
Printed by Aegean Offset Printers, Greater Noida, U.P.

ISBN 978-81-980002-7-9 (HB)

www.pentagonpress.in

Contents

Message by Ambassador Sandeep Chakravorty vii

Message by H.E. Ina H. Krisnamurthi ix

Foreword xiii

Editor's Note xv

1. India and Indonesia: Torchbearers of the Bandung Spirit 1
Ambassador Sandeep Chakrovorty

2. Commemorating 75 Years of Indonesia-India Relations: Shaping the Trajectory of Indonesia-India Relations 10
René L Pattiradjawane

3. Indonesia and India 75 Years of Diplomatic Relations: Time to Step Out of Diplomatic Crease 21
Ambassador Gurjit Singh

4. Indonesia: Not a Distant Neighbour but a Sibling of India, an Indic Family Member 34
Pulind Samant

5. India's Ancient Connections with Indonesia 45
Saudiptendu Ray

6. Indonesia-India Trade in Brief (1979-2022) 61
Akhmad Jayad

7. India and Indonesia: The Economic Potential 71
Sanjay Chadha

8. Defence Diplomacy between Indonesia and India to Maintain Maritime Security in the Indo-Pacific 80
Marina Ika Sari

9. Factoring ASEAN and IORA in Strengthening India-Indonesia Relations 91
Rahul Mishra

10. Finding Convergence for and Values in Indonesia-India Cybersecurity Capacity-Building 105
Mabda Haerunnisa Fajrilla Sidiq

11. Beyond Bilateralism: Strengthening India-Indonesia Ties within ASEAN 115
Dr Cchavi Vasisht

12. Evolving Geopolitical Dynamics of the Indo-Pacific Region and its Impact on India-Indonesia Relations 124
Vinod Anand and Faisal Ahmed

Index 136

AMBASSADOR
राजदूत

सत्यमेव जयते

INDIA @ 75

Message from Ambassador

I am indeed delighted that Vivekananda International Foundation in partnership with the Habibie Centre, Jakarta are jointly publishing a commemorative volume on Indo-Indonesia relations as both countries are commemorating the 75th anniversary of establishment of diplomatic relations.

2. India-Indonesian ties are not only age old but are also substantive and robust in the contemporary context. We align well both our foreign and economic policies. While India aspires to be a developed country, Viksit Bharat, by 2047, Indonesia is also aiming at achieving developed country status, Golden or Emas Indonesia by 2045. To achieve these goals both countries are embarking on pathways of achieving greater digitalisation, manufacturing, use of AI, food security, energy transition, nutrition, affordable health and leveraging the blue economy. These are also areas in which we can foresee greater India-Indonesia collaboration in the coming years. The strength and vibrancy of the India-Indonesia relationship will prove to be a key factor for stability in the Indo-Pacific.

3. Both are two countries are fortunate in enjoying the fruits of democracy. The leadership as well as the people of both the countries share mutual warmth and goodwill for each other. The sizable Indian diaspora and community in Indonesia also contributes in building bridges between the two countries.

4. I congratulate Vivekananda International Foundation for their initiatives to foster our bilateral ties and keep our ties on the radar by organising events from time to time. With the Habibie Foundation, we share a productive relationship and I visualise both these organisations providing the intellectual capital needed to sustain such a deep rooted and vibrant relationship.

(Sandeep Chakravorty)

भारत का राजदूतावास | EMBASSY OF INDIA
Embassy of India, Level 27 & 28, Gama Tower, Jl. H.R. Rasuna Said Kav. C-22, Jakarta - 12940, Indonesia.
दूरभाष / Phone : +62 21 2522 299
Website : www.indianembassyjakarta.gov.in • Email : amb.jakarta@mea.gov.in

Message by H.E. Ina H. Krisnamurthi
Ambassador of the Republic of Indonesia to the Republic of India

"INDIA-INDONESIA 75 YEARS ANNIVERSARY OF DIPLOMATIC RELATIONS: BUILDING BRIDGES BETWEEN THE PAST, PRESENT, FUTURE"

Congratulations to the Habibie Centre and Vivekananda International Foundation (VIF) for this Joint Publication in commemorating the 75th anniversary of diplomatic relations between Indonesia and India.

The diverse topics covered in this Joint Publication, indeed, highlight the depth of our partnership. This milestone allows us to reflect on our shared past, celebrate our accomplishments, and chart the path for a greater cooperation.

The Embassy's theme of the 75th anniversary is "Building Bridges between the Past, Present, and Future" captures the essence of our rich historical interactions spanning more than two millennia.

While our history provides a strong foundation, our partnership must continue to leap. Over the past 75 years, we have evolved from allies in the fight for independence to partners shaping the global order.

India's support during Indonesia's independence struggle from 1945 to 1949, the presence of President Soekarno as the chief guest of India's First Republic Day, and our initiative in convening the 1955 Bandung Conference remains a defining chapter in our relationship.

Today, we are emerging drivers of the Asian Century, with India and Indonesia key to regional stability and economic growth. As two of the world's largest democracies, both countries demonstrate that democracy thrives in pluralistic societies, as seen in our recent successful elections.

Since 2018, our ties have expanded into a comprehensive strategic partnership, spanning trade, defense, security, health, space, and people-to-people exchanges. We have also aligned our shared vision on maritime cooperation in the Indo-Pacific.

Defense cooperation emerge as among the key pillars in our bilateral relationship, formalized through the Defense Cooperation Agreement (DCA) and our maritime cooperation reflects our role as stewards of vital Sea Lines of Communication. In fact, we are just 90 nautical miles apart between Sabang and the Andaman & Nicobar Islands.

On economy, Indonesia is a significant trading partner for India within ASEAN, with bilateral trade reaching USD 38.85 billion in 2022-23 and Investment by each other's' countries rise steadily over time. People-to-people ties have grown exponentially, with nearly one million Indian citizens visiting Indonesia in 2023, and around 100 Memorandums of Understanding (MoUs) established between universities in both countries.

In the last 3 years, we celebrate many achievements, including the signing of the Local Currency Transaction (LCT) Agreement, direct flights between India and Indonesia, the India-Indonesia Track 1.5 Dialogue, and starting of Air Forces Talk.

With the succession in Indonesian Government with the inauguration of H.E. Prabowo Subianto as the President in October 2024, Indonesia's foreign policy would always be implemented on a solid foundation, namely the principles and values of free and active or "bebas aktif".

Furthermore, India and Indonesia's steadfast commitment to multilateralism have long been a cornerstone of their foreign policies, with both nations actively engage in international forums to address global challenges and promote cooperation. In 2022 and 2023 we both held the position of G20 Presidency consecutively and making us the Troika Presidency of G20 for two years in a row. Another historic moment in our bilateral relations was when India in 2023 held G20 Presidency, Indonesia was the Chair of ASEAN. We have strongly supported each other in this regard and contributed to each other successes of the chairmanships.

As our both countries share ambitious national visions, which are India's "Viksit Bharat 2047" and Indonesia's "Golden Indonesia 2045" to becoming fully developed nations by their independence centenaries, strengthening relations with India will remain a priority for Indonesia. Indonesia's "bebas aktif" and India's Act East Policy—serve as a strong basis to deepen our cooperation for the future.

Looking ahead, India and Indonesia are poised to become global economic powerhouses. Financial institutions project India and Indonesia to become among the five biggest economies in the world in 2030. As we confront with many inter-connected global challenges, Indonesia and India must continue to collaborate to achieve our 100 years anniversary's aspirations.

Lastly, I would like to, once again, extend my deepest gratitude to The Habibie Center, Vivekananda International Foundation, and all contributors for enriching this publication and enhancing our understanding on India-Indonesia relationship. The insights presented herein will certainly enhance our comprehension of the Indonesia-India relationship, and hopefully will stimulate innovative pathways for both countries' collaboration in the future.

Foreword

India and Indonesia are celebrating the 75th Anniversary of the establishment of their diplomatic relations in 2024. To commemorate the occasion, the Vivekananda International Foundation, New Delhi and the Habibie Centre, Jakarta have joined hands to hold a conference on India-Indonesia relations in New Delhi in November this year. We are delighted to publish the present volume on *India-Indonesian Relations: A Civilisational Partnership* which reflects on the past and assesses the future. Knowledgeable and experienced Indian and Indonesian scholars have contributed insightful and forward-looking articles to this volume.

I am grateful to H.E Sandeep Chakravorty, the Indian ambassador to Indonesia, for his article *India and Indonesia: Torchbearers of the Bandung Spirit* Special thanks are due to H.E Ina H. Krisnamurthi, the Indonesian Ambassador to India, for mooting the idea for the joint conference to celebrate the occasion and giving a message for the publication.

India and Indonesia are amongst the world's largest democracies and rising powers. As two civilisational states with a shared history going back to over two millennia, they are united by bonds of culture, shared history and people-to-people contacts. Prime Minister Nehru and President Sukarno were the driving force behind the historic Bandung Conference of 1955 which brought together the countries of Asia and Africa, gave a push to the decolonization process and gave shape to the Non-Aligned Movement during the Cold War years.

The contemporary global environment has changed since then. Wars, conflicts, climate change, the breakdown in the international order characterize today's turbulent world. New ideas are desperately needed to manage today's disorder. As the world's second and the fourth most populated countries respectively, close maritime neighbours and rising powers, India and Indonesia have the responsibility to work together for global, regional peace and stability. Given their past contribution to addressing regional and global issues, they are well placed to work together to voice the concern of the Global South in today's fragmented world. As Ambassador Sandeep Chakravorty points out in his insightful article, India and Indonesia should rekindle the Bandung Spirit in its new form to address contemporary issues.

The India-Indonesia relationship is unique. There is undeniably the nostalgia for the past. Pulind Samant in his article observes that Indonesia is not a distant neighbour but a 'sibling' of India and a member of the Indic family. This is an apt framework for our bilateral ties. The articles in the book recall Biju *Patnaik*'s heroics in 1948 in rescuing the Indonesian resistance leaders who were fighting the Dutch and bringing them to India in a plane he was piloting. There are also references to the warmth and bonhomie of the Nehru-Sukarno years. The relationship went through an indifferent phase subsequently and was revived in the 21st century after the fundamental political changes in Indonesia. The visits of the Indian Prime Minister to Jakarta in September 2023 and of the Indonesian President to India in Dec 2016 have opened up new vistas for the development of bilateral relations. Bilateral trade and investment are growing. India and Indonesia are also working towards strengthening the regional cooperation. A foundation has been laid to unlock the full potential of the bilateral relationship.

We hope that this publication will contribute to bringing the two countries and strategic communities closer and contribute towards a better understanding of each other's perspectives on a variety of issues and strengthen our relationship.

New Delhi
15 Oct 2024

Arvind Gupta
Director, VIF

Editor's Note

India and Indonesia both very close maritime neighbours, are celebrating their 75th anniversary of establishment of their diplomatic relations. It is also well recognised that both countries have ancient connections rooted in their historical and cultural past dating back to even before the Common Era. Both nations after suffering the adverse impact of colonialism became independent within two years of each other. Both nations were supportive of each other's struggle against the colonialism. India's and Indonesia's leaders like Nehru and Sukarno were at the forefront of organising the third world nations through Bandung Conference of April 1955 in Indonesia. This grouping gave rise to the formation of Non-Aligned Movement in 1961 that chose to stay away from the contestation between the then two power blocs. These were also the forerunners to the current South to South cooperation endeavours wherein India and Indonesia have been proactive.

Both nations with large populations are focussed on development and growth leading to betterment of their people. Prime Minister Modi on his visit to Indonesia in November 2022 for G20 summit had observed while addressing the diaspora in Bali on the sidelines of the summit that India and Indonesia are not 90 nautical miles apart but close thus underlining the closeness and depth of bilateral relationship. It also needs to be remembered that Indonesia had agreed to host the G20 Summit in 2022 on the request of India though it was India's turn then.

This joint publication between two premier think tanks of Indonesia and India explores various facets of bilateral relationship including both countries experiences with regional organisations including advancement of their mutual interests and objectives through cooperation with such groupings/organisations. The authors with their rich experience in international relations, political, economic and security issues as also in social and cultural interactions have lent their weight to the joint publication.

It is heartening to see that India's ambassador to Indonesia has contributed to the publication highlighting the need to maintain and nurture the Bandung Spirit as both countries are torchbearers of the same. Well experienced India's former Ambassador to Indonesia, Amb. Gurjit Singh has made several recommendations as to how best we can further deepen our bilateral relationship. Mr. Rene L Pattiradjawane writes a very perceptive essay on the bilateral relationship in the context of regional and global situations as also he expresses his views on the Chinese Dream. Development of economic relations, expanding of defence and security relationship, adhering to international norms and promoting peaceful and stable order remain the corner stones of our joint endeavours.

Pulind Samant has very rightly emphasised that Indonesia and India are not distant neighbours but siblings and members of Indic family. He goes into providing detailed evidences of how this is so and how Indonesia has extended its cooperation to India on various international forums including at the Organisation of Islamic Cooperation. Saudiptendu Ray dwells on India's Ancient Connections with Indonesia covering the Hindu and Buddhist linkages that led to creation of culture that was unique to the archipelago.

Akhmad Jayad and Sanjay Chadha in their well-researched article analyse the trade relations and economic potential of the bilateral relationship. Evidently, the full potential of bilateral trade and commerce is yet to be exploited. Several recommendations have been made to achieve the desired objectives e.g. continued collaboration in in infrastructure development, IT services, and electric vehicle technology to name a few areas of cooperation.

Cooperation in maritime domain has emerged as an essential facet of the bilateral relationship. Marina Ika Sari emphasises on Indonesia being the fulcrum connecting both Indian and Pacific Oceans and India occupying a central position in the Indo-Pacific. Marina also highlights the need for strengthening defence diplomacy between both the nations. Rahul Mishra expands on the such collaborative efforts and reflects on the role of ASEAN and IORA in strengthening bilateral relations.

Cyber security capacity building and collaboration between both the nations has been well explained by Mabda Haerunnisa Fajrilla Sidiq. Dr. Cchavi Vasisht has written on strengthening of bilateral relationship within the construct of ASEAN and lastly Prof Faisal Ahmed looks at the evolving dynamics of the Indo-Pacific region and its impact on the relations between Indonesia and India.

Overall, the edited volume covers multi-faceted aspects of India-Indonesian relations and coming at the 75th anniversary of diplomatic relations, it adds to the current discourse in a very useful way. Strengthening regional initiatives of both Indonesia and India resonates very well with the leadership of our two nations. I am sanguine that this publication will contribute towards better understanding of each other's perspectives on a variety of issues and strengthen our relationship.

October 2024

Vinod Anand
Editor

1

India and Indonesia: Torchbearers of the Bandung Spirit

*Ambassador Sandeep Chakravorty**

In April 2025, we will commemorate the 70th anniversary of the Asian-African Conference, popularly known as the Bandung Conference. The Conference was convened upon the invitations of the Prime Ministers of Burma, Ceylon, India, Indonesia, and Pakistan from April 18 to 24, 1955. In addition to the sponsoring countries, twenty-four more countries participated, including Egypt, P.R. China, and Gold Coast (Ghana). The Conference Communiqué detailed plans for a) economic cooperation; b) cultural cooperation; c) human rights and self determination; d) problems of dependent peoples; e) other problems which included the Palestine question; f) promotion of world peace and cooperation; and g) declaration on the promotion of world peace and cooperation. The last was articulated through ten principles which are still remembered in Indonesia as *Dasa Sila*.

It may not be an exaggeration to posit that the Bandung Conference is arguably the most transformative or impactful of international conferences ever, perhaps more than the San Francisco Conference of 1945 that led to the establishment of the UN. Not in terms of implementation of the Bandung Declaration, but the wide scale impact it had in the creation of new nation states and the influence it had on the UN itself. Bandung in many ways changed the face of the UN, and today, when there is greater salience of the Global South, it in many ways owes its origin to Bandung. The concept of the Third World or South emerged from Bandung. Although Bandung did not lead to

*Ambassador Sandeep Chakravorty is India's Ambassador to Indonesia.

the establishment of an international organisation or a secretariat, its impact on the UN was telling. By the end of 1955, sixteen new countries had become members of the UN. In 1960, 18 more countries became independent. As David Van Reybrouck points out in his masterly '*Revolusi*', the '*southernising*' of the UN happened. In 1961 more than half the members were from Asia and Africa, whereas in 1945 it had been less than a quarter. Bandung touched every continent. President Nasser of Egypt, upon his return from Bandung, unleashed henceforth unimaginable forces that greatly impacted the Arab world and Africa. The Suez crisis of October 1956 can be directly linked to moves made by Nasser, originating in Bandung. Kwame Nrumah of Ghana lit the flame even brighter.

Even Europe would not be the same after Bandung. While the conventional understanding is that the European project was a result of the need to prevent another war in Europe and it was a noble, internal peace mission, several authors project it differently. According to Peo Hansen and Stefan Jonsson in their work, "*Eurafrica: The Untold History of European Integration and Colonialism*", it arose as a reaction to what was happening in Asia and Africa. The unleashing of the forces of decolonisation made Europe vulnerable and strengthened the longing to combine Europe's forces to operate separately from both the US and the UN. This longing still continues and has only been marginally satisfied. European unification was meant to be a vigorous riposte to the anti-imperialism of the South. The mindset underlying Europe was late colonial, rather than post-colonial. So, while on one hand Bandung lit the decolonisation flame, on the other it warmed the need for European solidarity. Bandung even influenced the American Civil Rights movement. Barely eight months after the Conference, the Montgomery bus boycott had begun. African American author Richard Wright attended the Conference and his book *Color Curtain* was an eye opener on Bandung's moral imperatives.

The spirit of Bandung continued unabated till the mid-sixties when it got infected by Cold War dynamics and pioneers of the Afro-Asian movement all but disappeared. The post-Cold War era should have been a fertile environment for the rekindling of the Bandung spirit. However, the actors have changed. China has transformed remarkably and may no longer be considered as part of the Global South. This sets up the stage for greater India-Indonesia cooperation.

The Bandung Bonhomie

Coming out of colonial rule with the urge to play a leading role in global affairs, both India and Indonesia could boast of the highest level of diplomatic communication. It is a little-known fact that in December 1948, during 'Operation Crow' or what is known popularly as the Second Police Action by the Dutch colonial power to uproot the Republik from their stronghold in Yogyakarta, Sukarno had even contemplated the government of the nascent Republik would go into exile in India. It could not be realized as the Dutch took over the Yogyakarta airport. Such had been the level of mutual understanding between the leaders. Nehru, Hatta, Sjahrir had known each other for years. India constantly raised the Indonesian question in the UNSC. The Asian Relations Conference (ARC) in 1947 was purposely held to address the Indonesian question. Thanks to the heroics of Biju Patnaik, Sutan Sjahrir, the Prime Minister of the Republik was able to attend the ARC on the last day. President Sukarno was the Chief Guest at India's first Republic Day in 1950, and Nehru was Indonesia's first state guest. These bonds flourished and there was excellent strategic communication between Sukarno and Nehru which led to India joining hands with Indonesia and some other countries to convene the Bandung Conference. Nehru's participation in the Conference added much sheen and heft to the event. This collaboration amongst the star participants of the Bandung Conference – Sukarno, Nehru and Nasser, later led to the establishment of the Non-aligned Movement (NAM) in 1961 and the Group of 77 in 1964.

It is worthwhile to note that the *Dasa Sila* principles remain dear to both Indonesia and India and arguably form the basis of even their current foreign policy. Indonesia's 'free and active' foreign policy can be directly traced to *Dasa Sila*, while India's pursuit of strategic autonomy and not entering into any alliances or blocs can find basis in the outcome of Bandung.

Due to various reasons including cold war dynamics, the appearance of President Suharto on the scene in Indonesia, death of Nehru, India-China dynamics, India's Friendship Treaty with the USSR, the closeness between our two leaderships that propelled our ties after our respective independence, waned to some extent. With democracy taking firm roots in Indonesia in the early 2000s, the expectation for closer ties between India and Indonesia is well founded and has a genuine basis. India is the largest country by population and world's largest democracy. Indonesia is the fourth largest country in terms of population and the third largest democracy in the world. Our countries are held together by strong adherence to the belief in unity in diversity and acceptance of plurality is a part of our national ethos. *Bhinneka Tunggal Ika*, the national motto of Indonesia sounds incredibly familiar to Indian ears, whereas the import of Indian national motto - *Satyameva Jayate* is well understood in Indonesia (curiously it was recently even used as the theme of an event by a political party).

Both our countries are undergoing rapid economic transformation whilst enjoying the benefits of demographic dividend. While India aspires to be a developed country by 2047, Indonesia has similar aspirations as part of Indonesia *Emas* (Golden Indonesia) by 2045. The challenges we face are also quite similar in terms of food security, digitalisation, energy transition, and quality education and healthcare. It is not surprising that as part of his election manifesto, President Prabowo mentioned greater cooperation with India for achieving food security and launching the free school lunch scheme. There is also a conversation on replicating the success of Amul, which spurred India's White Revolution. Visits by Indonesian officials to Akshaya Patra kitchens have helped in formulating ideas for the school meals programme. There is admiration in Indonesia for the Food Corporation of India and the Public Distribution System which ensures food security for the marginalized. India's experience of food fortification is ready for uptake in Indonesia. There is considerable traction on the bilateral corridor with private sector companies wanting to increase their presence in each other's geographies. The bilateral exchange has been helped by the re-initiation of direct flight connectivity. It is unfathomable as to how till July 2023, there was no direct air connectivity linking India and Indonesia. At present, we have 21 flights a week and by the end of 2024, the much-needed air connectivity between our two capitals will be in place. Indonesia expects about a million Indian tourists in 2025, and some initial steps have already been taken to encourage medical tourism to India. Taking advantage of the change in law that now allows foreign hospitals to have partnership with local hospitals in SEZs, presence of Indian hospital groups in Indonesia will grow. The beginning is being made by the inauguration of the first such hospital in the new capital city of Nustantara (IKN) by Mayapada Hospitals teaming up with Apollo Hospitals. Our trade relations are substantive and in 2022-23 bilateral trade touched almost US$ 40 billion. While there has been a correction subsequently, still trade provides significant economic ballast to the relationship. The ASEAN-India Trade in Goods Agreement (AITIGA) of 2010 is presently under review. Upon its completion and when the cross-border digital payment inter-linkage and the mechanism for trade through Local Currency Settlement System (LCSS) is in place by the end of the year, the rails of economic integration will firmly be laid.

Rekindling Bandung

However, in the midst of noteworthy past and a healthy present state of relations, what may be lacking is greater diplomatic coordination and joint initiatives. Yohannes Sulaiman of Universitas Jenderal Achmad Yani, Cimahi, Indonesia in article published for the Indian think tank NatStrat in July 2024 concludes that "*the India-Indonesia relationship is at a crossroads, with both challenges and opportunities ahead. By leveraging their complementary strengths and addressing common challenges, both countries can enhance their bilateral cooperation. The comprehensive strategic partnership between India and Indonesia holds great potential for contributing to regional stability and prosperity in the Indo-Pacific region. At the same time, both countries can no longer maintain the status quo. Both Indonesia and India need to understand that many of their interests converge and thus need to continue taking initiatives to strengthen their relationship*". Can we relive and rekindle the Bandung spirit when we had joined hands to convene the epoch-making Conference whose reverberations still resonate?

India and Indonesia can and do work closely at a diplomatic level to achieve positive outcomes in multilateral forums. It is not only a lexical coincidence that we always sit next to each other on high tables. Intense diplomatic coordination was evident during Indonesia's presidency of G-20 in 2022 and India's presidency in 2023. At India's request, Indonesia even agreed to host the G-20 Summit in 2022 when it was our turn to do so. The back- to- back presidencies of Indonesia and India unleashed great dynamism in the relationship. Hosting the G-20 meetings in multiple towns across the countries helped in generating greater familiarity. The diplomatic coordination reached its peak with each of the two countries working closely in achieving a consensus 'Bali Declaration' and again, the consensus 'Delhi Declaration'.

Both India's External Affairs Minister and the Indonesian Foreign Minister worked closely behind the scenes to ensure that consensus was reached despite the rift between the West and Russia-China on Ukraine. It even gave rise to a less known but close friendship between the two. This coordination continued during the Jakarta East Asia Summit in 2023 and the Delhi G-20 Summit. Prime Minister Modi made a special gesture to travel to Jakarta to attend the ASEAN-India and the East Asia Summit in September 2023 just as foreign leaders were arriving in New Delhi for the G-20 Summit. There may also be other examples in the multilateral forums where both our countries coordinate positions. The question is can we do more and bigger on a continuous basis to make a visible impact. When was the last time that India and Indonesia jointly pioneered an initiative and took it to the world?

In 2015, India and France jointly launched the International Solar Alliance (ISA), conceived to mobilise efforts against climate change through deployment of solar energy solutions. It was conceptualised on the sidelines of COP 21 in Paris. Presently, the ISA has 124 members and is a solid testament to the strength of India-France ties. India has launched several other diplomatic initiatives to counter present day challenges such as the Coalition of Disaster Resilient Infrastructure (CDRI), the Global Biofuel Alliance (GBA) and International Big Cat Alliance (IBCA). The objectives and purposes of these initiatives fit well with Indonesia's national objectives of combating climate change and energy transition and its presence in these organisations will add value, and through joint efforts, will make them more vibrant.

The only regional organisation in which India and Indonesia both are partners is IORA. IORA is in a process of revitalisation which will bring it to the forefront of regional maritime diplomacy. India is a dialogue partner in ASEAN and while India-ASEAN ties are on an upswing as India commemorates the 10th anniversary of its Act East Policy, not being a member of the organisation has a circumscribing effect on efforts and results. In 2023, there was a buzz about Indonesia becoming part of BRICS. In 2024, the buzz has reappeared and Indonesia participating in the BRICS Summit at Kazan in October 2023, may open up possibilities. Another framework which syncs well with India and Indonesia being democracies and large economies of the global south is IBSA i.e. the India-Brazil-South Africa Dialogue Forum. Can Indonesia be included to make it IBSAI? Being active members of plurilateral frameworks unleashes energies which have a salutary impact on bilateral relations, as was seen during our G-20 presidencies, yet we share common membership of only a few.

It can be argued that the future of Asia could be decided by the strength of the India-Indonesia relationship, two countries who know how to navigate the trip wires of geo-politics. A multi-polar world can be ensured by a multi-polar Asia and for that to happen, India and Indonesia have to be strong and connected poles. The consensus G-20 Bali and Delhi Declarations are evidence of how the two countries are able to negotiate through the maze of competing claims and rival blocks. Yohannes Sulaiman describes India and Indonesia as unsatisfied middle powers, who aspire to be greater powers. The bigger role in global affairs that both India and Indonesia wish to play can possibly be realized more substantively through joint efforts. What could be the possible options?

Bandung 2.0

One option could be infusing more energy and dynamism in the mini-lateral frameworks. We have in place a nascent India-Indonesia-Australia framework. This could be tasked with more purpose and made responsible for joint activities in the maritime sphere. It could pick up a leaf or two from the Quad playbook in terms of ideas and projects with greater Indo-Pacific focus. In 2023, the India-Indonesia-Australia trilateral maritime exercise took place and we have also had maritime workshops in 2024. Could this be a harbinger for greater cooperation in the maritime sphere including HADR and curtailing IUU Fishing?

There is also the fledging India-Malaysia-Thailand Growth Triangle (IMT-GT). This could be the seed for closer sub-regional cooperation. The Aceh-Andaman Connectivity Initiative faces challenges. Being more integrated with IMT-GT could bring more wind to its sails. Joint development of Sabang Port in Aceh has been an idea for many years. Perhaps moving it from an idea to implementation can prove to be the building block for a new invigorated regional economic architecture. India is also interested in joining the Malacca Straits Patrol (MSP). Indonesia facilitating India joining the MSP will bring the countries closer together. Recently, BIMSTEC changed its charter allowing admission of new members. Indonesia is a Bay of Bengal littoral with interests in the Andaman Sea. Thailand is a member of BIMSTEC. Making Indonesia a member of BIMSTEC could be a diplomatic project of priority. Obviously, Indonesia will assess the benefits of being part of BIMSTEC. This could be part of the discussions during the accession process. Indonesia has also joined the Maritime Resources pillar of India's Indo-Pacific Oceans Initiative. It is incumbent on both the countries to ensure activities on the pillar through Blue Economy projects.

While India and Indonesia are on the opposite sides of the debate on UNSC expansion, even here there could be possibility of a united stance derived out of mutual accommodation. President José Ramos Horta of Timor-Leste is a big proponent of India and Indonesia occupying two permanent seats in an expanded UNSC. Could this idea result in yet another combined effort?

Parallel to India's G-20 presidency, India took the initiative of organising the Voice of Global South Summits (VOGSS). These were consultative meetings which enabled India to populate the G-20 agenda with the priorities of the Global South. President Joko Widodo participated in the 2nd VOGSS. Once again, South-South Cooperation is a priority as the Global South is not interested in getting mired in geopolitical conflicts which are affecting their food and fuel securities. Indonesia is also taking a lead in increasing its ties with the Global South. The Indonesia Africa Forum (IAF) was held in September 2024 in Bali which provides the pathway for greater Indonesian involvement with Africa. Could joint leadership of South-South Cooperation and taking care of the interests of the Global South be the glue which will bind us closer together?

India and Indonesia have a strong trading relationship and a growing investment relationship. Many Indian corporates are present in Indonesia (by the last count the number of Indian headquartered companies in Indonesia is about 100) and Indonesian companies have also started investing in India in more diversified areas. As the AITIGA review progresses, could India and Indonesia look at a bilateral Preferential or Free Trade Agreement or a Comprehensive Economic Partnership Agreement on the lines of India's agreement with Singapore? Bilateral trade negotiations somehow impart great energy to the ties and capture the imagination of people as several stakeholders get involved. Many start taking interest in the relationship as the author has personally witnessed during India's FTA negotiations with the UK and EU during the last few years. Perhaps initiating bilateral trade negotiations may provide the spark!

The task of any foreign policy is to ensure a congenial external environment to facilitate domestic transformation. For both India and Indonesia, the external environment is challenging, evolving and dynamic, impacting even domestic policies. So, whether it is to mitigate the effects of climate change, traditional and non-traditional security threats including cyber security, ensuring food and medicines for the population, and at the same time building national resilience, the task is enormous. It can become easier to fulfill it by joining hands with countries that are on the same side of the equation and have similar domestic and foreign policy orientations. The cooperative and transformative vision that existed at the time of Bandung Conference needs recreation. There are no other two countries that carry the intellectual and political legacy of Bandung than India and Indonesia and it enjoins on them to impart it with new meaning. For this our diplomatic establishments have to work closer together. A beginning was made in September 2024 by the initiation of a track bilateral 1.5 dialogue. Suggestions emerged for regular 2+2 meetings involving Foreign and Defence Ministers as well as annual Summits. All this and more are needed for Bandung 2.0. We are all aware of the existence and endurance of the Bandung Spirit. The challenge and task ahead for both countries is to give a new body to that spirit.

2

Commemorating 75 Years of Indonesia-India Relations: Shaping the Trajectory of Indonesia-India Relations

*René L Pattiradjawane**

"Nescire autem quid ante quam natus sis acciderit, id est semper esse puerum" (Not to know what happened before you were born is to be a child forever. For what is the time of a man except it be interwoven with that memory of ancient things of a superior age?) (Cicero, Orator 34.120)

> We are its products and we live immersed in it. Not to understand it and feel it as something living within us is not to understand the present. To combine it with the present and extend it to the future, to break from it where it cannot be so united, to make of all this the pulsating and vibrating material for thought and action—that is life. (Jawaharlal Nehru, *Discovery of India*, New York: Oxford University Press, 1946, 9)
>
> "Learning without thinking is useless, but thinking without learning is very dangerous." - Soekarno, Speech on Independence Day, August 17, 1961

Understanding the 75-year-long diplomatic relationship between Indonesia and India may not be enough to fully assess the broader relationship between both nations, which are geographically separated by the Indian Ocean. "People generally see what they look for and hear what they listen for." This phrase shows the Indonesia-India relationship, which reached 75 years in 2024, providing its own beliefs and perceptions of these two countries and how they position themselves in the dynamic regional-cum-global environment.

*René L Pattiradjawane is an Associate Fellow, The Habibie Center.

Although there is no direct evidence of Indian traders presence in Indonesian territory, Dutch scientists, conducting a study of Indonesian philological historiography, claim knowledge of Indians entering Indonesia, people visiting and an exchange of ideas between Indonesia and India, suggesting that this had occurred before Hinduism's entry into Indonesia in ancient times.[1]

Several inscriptions show that the first traces of Hindus were found in the western part of Java Island. This may be considered the oldest mention of Java, with the appearance of the name "Labadiou" in the book Geographical Hyphegesis written by Ptolemy (as the lost region of Java, where the word Labadiou in Sanskrit is identical to Yawadwipa).[2] According to Krom, there is uncertainty whether the mention of the embassy in 132, as the oldest Chinese report refers to, is the region of Java. If true, this means that the name mentioned is the country known to Hindus by this Indian name, not that they have settled there permanently. This can be concluded from the oldest Western Java inscriptions. The inscriptions are entirely Hindu; the language is Sanskrit and the script is Pallawa from the old homeland (India).[3]

The relationship between Indonesia and India is a multifaceted tapestry spanning millennia, woven with threads of history, culture, religion and commerce. From the earliest days of maritime trade to the contemporary challenges of a globalised world, these two nations have shared a unique bond rooted in mutual respect and understanding.

The relationship between both countries has a rich and intriguing history that spans centuries, from the earliest interactions of Indian traders sailing to the Indonesian archipelago to the present-day bilateral strategic and economic partnership. The influence of Hinduism and Buddhism, the absence of Hindu colonialism, the political, cultural, religious, financial, economic and military ties, and the importance of the Indian and Pacific Oceans in shaping this relationship, are all crucial aspects that deserve comprehensive analysis.

This essay explores the multifaceted interactions between both nations, tracing their journey from ancient times to modern. The bond between Indonesia and India is not just a bilateral relationship, but a significant element in broader regional and global politics. The early exchanges between Indonesia and India laid the foundation for a profound cultural and religious influence, primarily through the spread of Hinduism and Buddhism. Temples like Borobudur and Prambanan are monumental testaments to this historical connection. Unlike the colonial endeavours of European powers, Indian influence in Indonesia was characterised by cultural and religious integration, rather than political domination.

As we delve into the historical background, it becomes evident that Indonesia and India's political, cultural and economic interactions have evolved significantly over the centuries. The relationship has been dynamic and resilient, ranging from mutual support during their struggles for independence, to modern-day collaboration in various fields. The cultural exchanges, mainly through literature, art and religion, have left an indelible mark on both societies.

In the contemporary era, the Indonesia-India relationship has expanded to include strategic partnerships in politics, economics, and defence cooperation. Both countries are key players in regional organisations like ASEAN and the Indian Ocean Rim Association (IORA), and their collaboration extends to global platforms like the G-20. Their economic ties have been strengthened through significant bilateral trade and there is a growing emphasis on defence and security cooperation. Looking ahead, the Indian and Pacific Oceans hold immense geopolitical significance for both nations. These vast bodies of water facilitate trade and economic exchanges while playing a crucial role in ensuring maritime security. As Indonesia and India navigate 21st century complexities, their relationship will be pivotal to shaping the future of the Global South.

Reinvented

With its rich history dating back to the first century AD, India has long been a significant player in the global economic landscape. As the country has navigated the complexities of its political and economic development, it has emerged as an ambitious contender, determined to challenge China's dominance and establish itself as a major economic force.

Renowned British economist Angus Maddison's seminal work comprehensively analyses India's economic trajectory over the centuries.[4] Maddison's research reveals that India was once a thriving trade center, maintaining robust economic ties with its global partners. During the early centuries AD, India's GDP per capita was on par with that of Western Europe, a testament to its economic prowess. However, the country's fortunes dipped as it encountered the colonial era, with the British Empire's incursion leading to a significant decline in economic standing.[5]

Despite these historical setbacks, India has reinvented itself, emerging as a formidable economic force in the modern era. The country's rapid industrialisation, technological advancements and a burgeoning service sector contributing to its economic resurgence. As India sets its sights on surpassing China as one of the world's economic powerhouses, it faces a multitude of challenges, both internal and external.

Maddison's analysis provides a comprehensive understanding of India's economic evolution. His work highlights India's prominence as a central trading hub. Its sustained economic prowess can be traced back to its early interactions with various trading partners, including the Middle East, Southeast Asia and Europe. As India's economy expanded, it inevitably competed with the economic superpowers of the time, such as the United States and the European nations.

India's economic ambitions have been fueled by its sheer size, population and diversity of resources. Maddison notes, "India's share of world GDP was as high as 23% in the year 1 AD, declining to 3% in 1950, but recovering to over 5% by 2010."[6] This remarkable trajectory underscores the country's resilience and determination to reclaim its former economic glory.

However, India's ambition to become the world's strongest economic power, in competition with China, has its challenges. In the next decade, India will face significant economic and financial challenges, such as addressing infrastructure deficiencies, skill gaps and regulatory bottlenecks. These issues and the ongoing rivalry with China will require India to implement strategic reforms, invest in critical sectors and leverage its unique demographic dividends to solidify its position as a global economic force.[7]

Furthermore, India's ambition to outpace China economically is complicated by the latter's formidable economic prowess. China has emerged as a global manufacturing powerhouse and a key player in international trade, posing a formidable challenge to India's aspirations. Despite these obstacles, India remains steadfast in its pursuit of economic supremacy. As the country continues to implement strategic reforms, invest in critical sectors and leveraging its demographic dividends, it is poised to solidify itself as a global economic force. The journey, however, is not without complexities, and India must navigate the treacherous waters of international competition and domestic challenges to realise its ambitious vision for the future.

Rippling Effects

India's economic and trade development, characterised by rapid growth and a burgeoning middle class, is poised to send ripples across the global financial landscape, with significant implications for Southeast Asian nations like Indonesia. While the relationship between both countries holds immense potential for mutually beneficial partnerships, it also presents challenges that warrant careful consideration.

One of the most significant impacts of India's economic rise on Indonesia will be felt in the realm of trade. As India's economy expands, so will its demand for goods and services, including those that Indonesia is well-positioned to provide. With its abundant natural resources, including palm oil, coal and minerals, Indonesia could witness increased demand from India, potentially boosting its export sector and contributing to its economic growth.

Over the past two decades, the Indian economy has experienced a remarkable growth, with its GDP expanding at an average annual rate of over six percent.[8] This rapid economic development has significantly impacted the global economic landscape, where its influence has been particularly felt in Southeast Asia, including Indonesia. Indonesia, as the largest economy in Southeast Asia, has a complex and multifaceted relationship with India, and the ongoing economic and trade dynamics between the two countries is of critical importance to the region's future.

India has become a significant trading partner for Indonesia, with bilateral trade reaching USD 32.7 billion in 2022, an increase from the previous year's USD 21 billion.[9] This trade relationship is expected to grow further, with both countries seeking to expand their economic cooperation, particularly in the energy, infrastructure and manufacturing sectors.

For Indonesia, India's economic growth presents both opportunities and challenges. On the one hand, India's growing economy represents a potentially lucrative market for Indonesian exports, particularly in sectors like agriculture, mining and manufacturing. Additionally, India's expertise in IT and pharmaceuticals can provide valuable opportunities for collaboration and knowledge transfer.

However, India's economic rise also poses potential challenges for Indonesia. As India's manufacturing sector expands, it could increase competition for Indonesian firms in global markets. Moreover, India's growing demand for energy and natural resources could put upward pressure on prices, potentially impacting Indonesia's energy security and economic stability.

In conclusion, India's economic growth over the past two decades has been remarkable, driven by many factors, including a burgeoning services sector, a large and youthful population, and economic liberalisation. While this economic rise presents both opportunities and challenges for Indonesia, India's growing economy will likely continue to shape the economic and geopolitical landscape of the region for years. As India continues on its path of economic growth and development, it will be crucial for both her and Indonesia to navigate these complex dynamics carefully and work together to foster a mutually beneficial relationship that contributes to the region's overall prosperity.

Pivotal Role

Seventy years ago, in 1954, the Prime Ministers of Burma, India, Indonesia, Pakistan and Sri Lanka met and began a process that would transform history. This process led to the 1955 Bandung Conference, a transformative and pivotal event that proclaimed the Ten Principles, ushering in a new era of universal standards and norms based on independence, justice, and equity.[10]

India's active support was instrumental in shaping Indonesia's path to sovereignty by advocating for its independence on the global stage, particularly at the United Nations.[11] This support, along with the collective efforts of the Colombo Powers,[12] significantly contributed to securing recognition of Indonesia's sovereignty. This collaborative endeavour culminated in the historic Asia-Africa Conference in Bandung, Indonesia, in 1955, giving momentum to the Non-Aligned Movement.[13]

The pivotal role played by India in supporting Indonesia's struggle for sovereignty against The Netherlands cannot be overstated. As Indonesia fought for its hard-won independence, India's diplomatic efforts and unwavering support in the international arena proved instrumental in amplifying Indonesia's voice and securing its rightful place among the community of nations.

Sukarno, Indonesia's charismatic leader, and Nehru, India's first Prime Minister, shared a common vision for a world free from colonial shackles. Their rapport transcended mere diplomatic pleasantries, evolving into a deep-seated friendship that laid the foundation for a robust bilateral partnership. This camaraderie was instrumental in shaping the early years of Indonesia-India relations, fostering an atmosphere of mutual respect and cooperation.[14]

The Bandung Conference was a watershed moment in the history of Indonesia-India relations, as the two nations grappled with the complex issues surrounding the emerging Non-Aligned Movement.[15] The debates and discussions within this forum shed light on the nuanced positions held by Sukarno and Nehru, both revered as champions of national sovereignty and anti-colonial sentiment.[16] The ensuing conflicts and disagreements between the two leaders, particularly concerning the Cold War dynamics and Sukarno's perception of neo-colonialism, further underscored the delicate balance of power and influence that shaped the evolving relationship between the two neighbours.

Sukarno and Nehru's differences over the Cold War and Sukarno's perception of neo-colonialism complicated the bilateral relationship as both leaders sought to assert their respective visions for the region and the global order.[17] The influence of Socialist and Communist countries, particularly the Soviet Union and China, also significantly shaped the dynamics between Indonesia and India, as both sought to balance their relations with these ideological and geopolitical powers.

The complex interplay of these regional and global forces, coupled with the personal dynamics between the political elites of the two countries, left an indelible mark on the trajectory of Indonesia-India relations. As both grappled with maritime issues and navigated the shifting sands of regional power dynamics, the legacy of this period continued to shape the nuances of their bilateral engagement.

Conclusion

Since the tragic events of the terrorist attack in Washington and New York in September 2001, Western countries have taken grave missteps. Questionable interventions in Iraq, Afghanistan and Libya have tarnished their global standing. The 2008 economic crisis was not only a global disaster, but it also deeply shook the trans-Atlantic sphere, while countries like China, Indonesia and India continued to thrive. We have sent the wrong message to non-democratic states for too long, suggesting that democracy is unreliable and fragile. This emphasizes the urgent need for a more resilient and dependable democratic system. While democracy has always been known for its deliberation, it can also evidently allow for severe misjudgments. In light of these events, it is reasonable to question as to which country would look towards today's United States as a model of democracy.

In contemporary discussions, there has been a growing focus on the maritime security arrangement in the Indian and Pacific Oceans as an emerging geopolitical consideration of the 21st century. The unpredictable dynamics in regional hotspots like the Korean Peninsula and the Middle East have led us to reflect on our collective ability to establish genuine peace, greater stability and common progress in the region, particularly in Asia and Southeast Asia. Over the years, substantial and ongoing endeavours have been dedicated to addressing these diverse obstacles that impede the fulfilment of this shared aspiration, demonstrating our unwavering commitment to this cause.

Maritime diplomacy has assumed new importance in the second decade of the 21st century, especially in Asia. It is vital in shaping relationships between Asian nations and those outside the region. The concept of a maritime mandala has paved the way for a new era, presenting opportunities not just to prevent direct conflicts through modern naval capabilities and information technology but also to promote cooperation among Asian nations. In the current era of globalisation, countries' interdependence, complex economic and trade mechanisms and interactions with various states are essential in advancing each nation's national interests.

In the Asian and Southeast Asian context, we observe a unique situation where global powerhouses like the US, Japan and China compete economically and militarily. This has sparked a new era of uncertainty in the Asia-Pacific region. The increased arms race among Asian nations further underscores the tension and potential risks. India is on the brink of becoming a significant regional powerhouse, ready to contest spheres of influence and establish alliances in anticipation of possible shifts resulting from the new leader in Washington's decision to abandon the Trans-Pacific Partnership agreement in favour of a more sophisticated trade arrangement.

China, as a formidable force in the new world order, is strategically positioned to establish a "Chinese Century" that will surpass the historical influence of the "British Century" and the "American Century." This strategic positioning instils confidence in China's potential to achieve absolute dominance in the military arena and economics, trade, finance, and information technology. These achievements are crucial for revitalising China's historical legacy, known as the "Chinese dream," which connects the country's past with its future potential.

By 2030, the "Chinese dream" touted by Communist Party leader Xi Jinping, will no longer hold sway. Like the "Washington Consensus" of unfettered financial forces, Beijing's authoritarian state capitalism will have lost its allure. China, India and Brazil must forge their development models as Western approaches may not directly apply. These nations must prioritise environmental concerns and fortify their institutions in response to heightened citizen awareness. Russia faces daunting prospects, grappling with a declining population, an economy heavily reliant on commodities and widespread civic disillusionment.

When examining the security environment in the Asia-Pacific region, it is imperative to acknowledge and understand the three levels of relationships. The first level involves interactions among countries within the sub-region of Southeast Asia. The second level encompasses the relationships between Southeast Asian countries and their neighbours in the wider East Asia/West Pacific region, particularly the major powers that significantly influence this region. Finally, the third level includes the relationships among the four major powers—China, Japan, Russia and the US—as they interact globally and regionally. This robust framework provides a thorough and confident approach to comprehending and addressing regional security dynamics.

In summary, the initial years of Indonesia-India relations were characterised by a nuanced interplay of shared aspirations, personal connections between leaders, and evolving geopolitical dynamics. While the initial camaraderie laid a robust foundation for bilateral ties, Cold War complexities, ideological differences and aspirations for leadership in the Asia-Africa region introduced challenges. Nevertheless, the historical ties, particularly the shared experiences, played a significant role in shaping the trajectory of Indonesia-India relations in the subsequent decades.

NOTES

1 Krom,N.J.. *Hindoe-Javaansche Geschiedenis.* (*Hindu-Javanese History*), ('S-Gravenhage: Koninklik Instituat voor de Taal-, Land- en Valkerkunde van Ned-Indie, Martinus Nijhoff, 1926), p. 34-62. According to Dr Christine Elizabeth Dobbin, an Indonesianist who graduated from Oxford University, the archipelago area already known by Indian traders is the Rao Valley area in the Minangkabau area, which has a long tradition of dealing with the whole world. The Rao region is an important gold mining region in Minangkabau, and Indian traders have known the gold trade since the beginning of the second century AD. It is mentioned that there are about 800 Indian settlements around the Rao Valley; in the 18th century, Rao's gold reserves were never exhausted. The gold trade from Rao was exported, continuously filling ship traffic in the Malacca Strait. Look at Dobbin, Christine. *Islamic Revivalism in a Changing Peasant Economy: Central Sumatra 1784-1847,* (London and Maimô, Curzon Press Ltd, 1983), p. 176

2 See https://kekulturaan.kemdikbud.go.id/bpcbjambi/visiting-suwarnabhumi-negeri-kaya-logam-mulia-3/, accessed August 20, 2024

3 Krom,N.J.. *Hindoe-Javaansche Kunst.* (*Hindu-Javanese Art*), ('S-Gravenhage: Martinus Nijhoff, 1923), pp. 51-52.

4 Maddison, Angus. *Contours of the World Economy, 1–2030 AD: Essays in Macro-Economic History,* (Oxford: Oxford University Press, 2007)

5 Maddison, Angus. *The World Economy: A Millennial Perspective,* (Paris: OECD, 2001, p. 85-117)

6 Maddison, 2007, ibid, pp. 118-131

7 Ahluwalia, Isher Judge & Little, I.M.D. (ed.). *India's Economic Reforms and Development: Essays for Manmohan Singh* (New Delhi: Oxford University Press, 1998)

8 India GDP Annual Growth Rate, https://tradingeconomics.com/india/gdp-growth-annual, accessed 1 September 2024

9 Although India managed to rank fifth, shifting the UK as a world economic power after the US, China, Japan, and Germany, because its large population caused its per capita income to be still low (US$ 2,500) compared to the UK (US$ 47,000). "India Overtakes U.K. to Become Fifth Largest Economy in the World," *The Hindu*, 3 September 2022, https://www.thehindu.com/news/national/india-overtakes-uk-to-become-fifth-largest-economy-in-the-world/article65844906.ece, accessed 21 August 2024

10 Anak Agung Gde Agung, Ide. *Twenty years Indonesian foreign policy 1945–1965.* (Berlin, Boston: De Gruyter Mouton, 1973), pp. 193-247, https://doi.org/10.1515/9783111558226

11 Wilcox, Francis O. "The Nonaligned States and the United Nations," in Martin, Laurence W. (ed.) *Neutralism and Nonalignment: The New States in World Affairs.* ((New York: Frederick A. Praeger). 1962, pp. 121-151

12 Ewing, Cindy. "The Colombo Powers: crafting diplomacy in the Third World and launching Afro-Asia at Bandung." *Cold War History*, Volume 19, Issue 1 (2019), p. 1-19. . https://doi.org/10.1080/14682745.2018.1500553

13 Jansen, G. H. *Nonalignment and the Afro-Asian States.* (New York and Washington, Frederick A. Praeger, 1966).

14 Benvenuti, Andrea. *Nehru's Bandung: Non-Alignment and Regional Order in Indian Cold War Strategy.* (London, N.p.: Hurst Publishers, 2024. C. Hurst & Co. (Publishers) Ltd., 2024

15 Jansen, *ibid*

16 Barnett, A. Doak. "Asia and Africa in session: Random notes on the Asian-African Conference." (Surabaja: American Universities Field Staff, 18 May 1955), pp. 1–36.

17 Singh, L.P. "Dynamics of Indian-Indonesian Relations." *Asian Survey*, Vol. 7, No. 9 (September, 1967), pp. 655-666. doi: https://doi.org/10.2307/2642622

3

Indonesia and India 75 Years of Diplomatic Relations: Time to Step Out of Diplomatic Crease

Ambassador Gurjit Singh

India and Indonesia are two neighbours with many similarities. A strong ancient cultural connection binds them together. Trade, religion and social contact were initiated by early traders from Indian states with their counterparts in the kingdoms of Java and Sumatra. Nalanda and Muara Jambi were advanced universities linked through scholarship.

India and Indonesia are among the world's largest democracies and countries with the largest Muslim populations, which are youthful, aspirational, and committed to development. Both are members of the G20, the Non-Aligned Movement (NAM), the East Asian Summit (EAS) and similar other organisations. Both completed their journey towards independence after the end of World War II and shared common aspirations of freedom and nationhood.

The Initial Years: 1949-1966

Despite such similarities and the geographical closeness between the Andamans and Aceh state in Sumatra, the distance in the mind between Jakarta and New Delhi has been rather difficult to bridge. The popularity of the Ramayana and the Mahabharata in Indonesia and their adaptation into their own cultures, even after adopting a Muslim identity, is unique. Despite this common heritage, India and Indonesia have the 'Masala Bumbu' effect, where they often say similar sounding things but don't always understand each other.[1]

*Ambassador Gurjit Singh is a Former Ambassador of India to Indonesia.

'Masala Bumbu' refers to the fact that masala in Hindi means spice, while bumbu means the same in Bahasa Indonesia. However, masala in Indonesian also means an issue or a problem. In some ways, the problem of spices divided India and Indonesia, which were otherwise linked in antiquity through active trade and socio-economic ties. The onset of colonialism with the British in India and the Dutch in Indonesia saw them pursue the spice trade, among other things, with great enthusiasm. Their rivalries separated India and Indonesia from their common heritage.

When Japan capitulated on August 15, 1945, after occupying Indonesia, Sukarno spearheaded an immediate declaration of Indonesia's independence. The Allies sent the Dutch back to Indonesia to run it, leading to a forceful campaign for independence. Indonesia formally became independent on August 17, 1949, though they count their independence from August 1945. Indian independence took place on August 15, 1947. India held two conferences: one on Asian Relations (March-April 1947) and the other on Indonesian independence (January 1949), for both of which, Indonesian leaders were sent by Sukarno.

Sukarno wrote to Nehru on August 19, 1946, saying, "Your country and your people are linked to us by ties of blood and culture, which date back to the very beginning of history. The word 'India' must be a part of our life, for it forms the first two syllables of the name we have chosen for our land and race—the 'Indo' in Indonesia."[2]

The legendary role of the late Biju Patnaik came into prominence when he flew his aircraft into the provisional Indonesian government headquarters in Yogyakarta. Despite Dutch attacks, he successfully flew out then Prime Minister Sutan Sjahrir to attend the Asian Relations Conference (ARC) in New Delhi. Remarkably, the ARC is not listed among the important events on the website of the Indonesian Ministry of Foreign Affairs.[3]

Post-Independence Partnership: Nehru and Sukarno

Once both countries became independent, the Nehru-Sukarno partnership and friendship intensified. They focussed on how both countries could develop for the benefit of their people. In 1946, Indonesia sent rice to support India and India reciprocated by sending medicines to assist Indonesia.

In 1950, when India became a republic, the first chief guest at the Republic Day function was Sukarno, accompanied by his wife, Fatmawati. This was considered natural, given the close historical and emerging post-colonial ties between India and Indonesia. Their collaboration was evident among the Colombo Powers, which included Pakistan, Ceylon and Burma, focusing on these issues in an Asian context. India initiated scholarships for Indonesian and Burmese students, benefitting talented individuals like Indonesian artist Affandi, who came with a personal recommendation from Sukarno to Nehru. Affandi's exceptional skills led to his scholarship being transferred to his young daughter, Kartika, with whom we had the good fortune of celebrating her 80th birthday in Yogyakarta, where she fondly remembered her early days in Shantiniketan. In June 1950, Nehru's celebrated journey to Indonesia on INS Delhi highlighted the geographical proximity and close relations between both countries.

Nehru also visited Indonesia for the Bogor Conference in December 1954, for the Colombo Powers summit, and in April 1955, for the Bandung Conference.

Nehru and Sukarno were closely connected during the post-independence period, with Nehru providing support to Indonesia's struggle for independence. Indonesia awarded Nehru its highest honour for his support, which had helped Indonesia stop Dutch attempts to regain control.

The Bandung Conference and the Non-Aligned Movement

India and Indonesia, supported by the Colombo Powers, took the lead in organising an Afro-Asian conference. After a meeting in Bogor in 1954, they led to the Bandung Afro-Asian Conference in 1955. This conference marked a high point in India-Indonesia relations, as they promoted a development-focussed partnership for the benefit of other nations emerging from colonialism.[4]

The invitation to China to attend the Bandung Conference created some fissures among participants, compounded by domestic pressures in both countries. India received more Soviet aid, while Sukarno faced pressure from the Communist Party. Despite both countries being founding members of the Non-Aligned Movement, differences in their approach to development emerged by the time of the 1961 summit in Belgrade. These differences were not easily reconciled.

Strategic Shifts and Divergence

Indonesia remained neutral during the 1962 Sino-Indian conflict, but by 1965, during the India-Pakistan conflict, Sukarno's Indonesia was strategically aligned with Pakistan. By 1966, Sukarno was deposed, and India transitioned through the Nehru and Shastri eras to the Indira Gandhi era. The next decade saw both countries preoccupied with domestic politics, with the memory of their divergence in the Non-Aligned Movement buttressed by two other factors.

First, India supported Indonesia on the issue of West Irian (the Indonesian province of Papua), viewing it as part of decolonisation. However, Indonesia was displeased with India for not fully supporting it in its confrontation with Malaysia in Borneo, due to India's Commonwealth link with Malaysia. Indonesia possibly used this as a reason to support Pakistan in 1965.

Secondly, the military government in Indonesia viewed India as more of a Soviet Union supporter, while the Suharto-led New Order aligned with the US, particularly in the context of the Vietnam War. Indonesia broke diplomatic relations with China between 1967-1990, complicating its regional relations.

The New Order Period (1966-1998)

During the New Order period, Indonesia and India had different worldviews due to their regional contingencies and geographical proximity no longer playing a significant role in their relationship. The New Order period, spanning from 1966 to 1998 under President Suharto, marked a complex and transformative era in Indonesian history. This witnessed significant internal consolidation and economic growth in Indonesia, as well as shifts in its foreign policy. For India, the New Order represented a time of reevaluating its relationship with Indonesia amidst changing geopolitical dynamics.

Under Suharto's leadership, Indonesia underwent extensive political and economic changes. The New Order regime focussed on stabilising the country after the political turmoil of the mid-1960s, emphasizing economic development and attracting foreign investment. This led to rapid industrialisation and significant improvements in infrastructure, health and education.

In terms of foreign policy, Suharto's regime aligned with Western powers, particularly the United States, reflecting its anti-Communist stance during the Cold War. This alignment was in contrast to India's non-aligned position and its perceived closeness to the Soviet Union, creating a divergence in their international outlooks.

The military-led New Order government saw India through a different lens compared to the Sukarno era. The regime's alignment with the United States during the Cold War contrasted with India's closer ties with the Soviet Union. This divergence was particularly evident during the Vietnam War, where Indonesia's concerns about regional stability were heightened by the US military presence and its eventual withdrawal in 1973.The launch of ASEAN in 1967 gave Indonesia a greater regional interface and a focus away from its original engagement with the Colombo Powers and India.

Despite these geopolitical divergences, both nations maintained a pragmatic approach to their bilateral relationship. Military-to-military contacts continued, albeit with varying intensity. The Indian and Indonesian navies participated in joint exercises, and there were regular exchanges of military delegations. These interactions helped build a foundation of trust and mutual understanding, which would later be essential to strengthening defence cooperation in the post-New Order era. Prime Minister Indira Gandhi paid a state visit in June 1969, but did not visit during her second term. Suharto visited India in 1980 to nudge the relationship forward. Mrs. Gandhi visited in September 1981 and it was followed up by the President N. Sanjeeva Reddy's visit in December 1981, in a year of many exchanges. Rajiv Gandhi also visited Indonesia in October 1986. In 1989, India and Indonesia were both part of the G15 group of developing countries for South-South Cooperation.

Economic Engagement and Challenges

Economically, the New Order period saw limited bilateral trade and investment between India and Indonesia. While Indonesia focussed on attracting Western and Japanese investments to fuel its economic growth, India was undergoing its own economic challenges and policy shifts. The economic liberalisation in India in 1991 provided new opportunities for engagement, but these were not fully realised until later.

Trade relations during the New Order period were primarily centered around basic commodities, with limited diversification. Indonesian exports to India mainly consisted of natural resources such as timber, rubber and oil, while India exported textiles, machinery and pharmaceuticals. Both countries recognised the potential for greater economic collaboration, but political and economic constraints limited substantial progress. Indian investment in Indonesia increased availing the more liberal and stable investment environment provided at that time.

After the Cold War ended, Suharto's human rights and democratic record attracted the attention of the West. He then turned more to NAM and also for economic reasons to the Asia Pacific Economic Cooperation (APEC). Indonesia became a founding member of APEC in 1989 and hosted the Bogor APEC Summit in 1994. Suharto chaired the NAM in 1992. This showed the twin track he followed in the later part of the new order. India was not in APEC, but since 1992, a Look East Policy was enunciated and a dialogue partnership with ASEAN was started. The opportunities for larger diplomatic interaction between India and Indonesia began growing. Prime Minister Narasimha Rao participated in the NAM Summit in Indonesia in 1992. In 1996, India joined the ASEAN Regional Forum (ARF) and upgraded its ASEAN engagement to a full Dialogue Partnership.

The New Order period was marked by significant internal consolidation in Indonesia and evolving geopolitical dynamics that influenced its relationship with India. While there were notable divergences in their international alignments, both countries maintained a pragmatic approach to bilateral relations, focusing on areas of mutual interest. The end of the New Order and the return of democracy in Indonesia opened a new chapter in India-Indonesia relations, characterised by intensified engagement and a shared vision for regional stability and development in a post-Cold War world.

The legacy of the New Order period, with its complex interplay of cooperation and divergence, continues to shape the contemporary India-Indonesia relationship. As both nations navigate the challenges and opportunities of the 21st century, the lessons from this period provide valuable insights into building a resilient and dynamic partnership.

Domestic and Foreign Policy Shifts in the Last 27 Years

The end of the New Order in 1998 saw Indonesia transitioning to a fledgling democracy, that has led to a more intense and diversified engagement with India over the last 27 years (1998-2024).

President Habibie (1998-1999) served as the transitional president after Suharto. He was succeeded by well-known religious leader Abdurrahman Wahid (Gusdur) (1999-2001), who was replaced mid-term by Vice President Megawati Sukarnoputri (2001-2004), the eldest daughter of founding President Sukarno. Megawati contested elections twice against her coordinating minister and former general Susilo Bambang Yudhoyono (SBY), who won and held the presidency for a decade from 2004 to 2014, coinciding with the two UPA governments in India.

The Return of Democracy

As the New Order was ending, the first three presidents had a broad internal consolidation agenda. In 1998, when Habibi took over as president on May 21, 1998, India had just conducted its nuclear tests on May 11 and 13. Indonesia was too involved in its own affairs as India dealt with sanctions and a new stature in the world.

While Gusdur made a visit to India as part of a multinational tour, his ill health prevented a major engagement. His visit was overshadowed by the threat of a military coup by General Wiranto who then had to be dismissed by the president upon his return. Wiranto became a political leader and was a minister in some governments thereafter. Several generals in Indonesia made the transition to civilian political rule. While SBY became president for two terms, General Prabowo has been elected president in 2024 and will be in office from October 2024 to 2029.

The India-Indonesia relationship got a bilateral fillip, when Megawati visited India in May 2002. It was during her time that the Indian summit partnership with ASEAN came to the fore. In 2002, India was invited to become a summit- level dialogue partner of ASEAN, essentially upgrading the 1996 Dialogue Partnership, Though Cambodia, the latest ASEAN member, was the ASEAN Chair at the time, it was essentially Indonesia under Megawati, which assumed the ASEAN presidency for 2003, and institutionalised this relationship with India.

The return of democracy to Indonesia, led them to wider understandings of India, particularly the India of the 21st century and engage with new warmth and openness, bringing them into linkages with ASEAN on whom now Indonesia placed much of its diplomatic practice. This aspect was continued under the SBY presidency.

When the East Asia Summit was established in 2005, some ASEAN members preferred the EAS to be an arrangement with China, Japan and Korea, which already existed as the ASEAN Plus Three (APT), but it was Indonesia and Singapore, which sought greater diversity and balance and, therefore, wanted India, Australia and New Zealand to be part of the EAS along with the APT. Thus, Indian engagement with the Asia-Pacific region was finally recognised. In this, Indonesia, during the SBY period, had a role to play.

This trend continued and when Indonesia chaired APEC in 2013, they made a definitive effort to bring India into APEC, supported by some others. By then Chinese assertiveness in the region had become aggressive. It was China's veto which prevented Indonesia from carrying forward the reopening of APEC membership, which had had a moratorium placed on it.

The point to emphasize is that modern Indonesia sees the partnership with India as a balancing of the region compared to other powers, be it the US or China.

Related to this is the intensity which has come to India-Indonesia relations bilaterally. The visits of presidents Gusdur and Megawati brought new ideas of cooperation forward. It was SBY, who visited India three times, including as chief guest at the Republic Day function in 2011, who brought diversity and depth to the engagement this visit. There were 11 agreements and 18 B2B MOUs signed for projects, investment and trade and a boom period for India and Indonesia was anticipated.[5] However, 14 of the 18 project MOUS were never implemented.[6] SBY had also visited India in 2005, when a Strategic Partnership was initiated, and in 2012, for the 20th anniversary Commemorative India-ASEAN Summit.

From India, Prime Minister Vajpayee visited Indonesia in January 2001 and later for the India-ASEAN Summit in October 2003. Dr Manmohan Singh attended the 50th anniversary of the Bandung Summit in April 2005, visited in 2011 for the ASEAN and EAS Summits, and in 2013, for a bilateral visit.

The Jokowi-Modi Period

In 2014, Joko Widodo (Jokowi) won the presidential election and served two terms until October 2024, coinciding with Narendra Modi's tenure in India. Despite early promises, the bilateral relationship did not develop as anticipated due to Jokowi's focus on infrastructure projects with China, sidelining other countries, including India. Nevertheless, trade and investment between India and Indonesia flourished, albeit with limited Indonesian investment in India.

The pro-China tilt in Jokowi's policy led to increased Chinese dominance in the Indonesian economy, particularly in mining and infrastructure sectors. Initially, Indonesia, like many ASEAN countries, underestimated China's aggressive intent in the South China Sea. However, Chinese intrusions into Indonesia's Exclusive Economic Zone (EEZ) in the Natuna Sea prompted a shift in perception.[7]

The 2004 tsunami saw the Indian Navy's swift and effective assistance to Indonesia, reinforcing Indonesia's view of India as a benign neighbour. By 2023, Indonesia was prepared to engage in maritime cooperation with India, as evidenced during the India-ASEAN meeting in September 2023. While bilateral MOUs on maritime security were not always necessary, ASEAN MOUs often facilitated regional cooperation without appearing to challenge China directly.

Indonesia valued its Bandung legacy and felt a protocol imbalance when Prime Minister Modi did not attend the 60th anniversary commemorations in 2015, despite an invitation from Jokowi. This absence was noted, although Modi had explained his prior commitments during a brief meeting at the funeral of Singapore PM Lee Kuan Yew.

Bilateral visits and summits continued to play a crucial role in strengthening India-Indonesia relations. Jokowi visited India in 2016, and although Modi's visit was delayed until 2018, subsequent engagements deepened cooperation. The Indian Ocean Rim Association (IORA) Summit in 2017 saw the Indian delegation led by the Vice President, highlighting the importance of regional cooperation.

The Act East Policy (AEP) of 2014, announced by Modi, emphasized a more focussed engagement with ASEAN, covering economic, political, strategic and socio-cultural pillars. This policy resonated with Indonesia, leading to enhanced bilateral and regional cooperation.

While the early promise of the Jokowi-Modi leadership did not fully materialise, frequent meetings at ASEAN, EAS and G20 Summits facilitated ongoing dialogue. Jokowi's preference for Chinese infrastructure investments impacted India's role in Indonesia's development projects, but trade and investment continued to grow.

Modern Indonesia views its partnership with India as a regional balancing act amidst the influence of other powers, particularly the US and China. The bilateral relationship has evolved with significant engagements, including the visits of presidents Gusdur, Megawati, SBY and Jokowi. Notable achievements include the strategic partnership initiated in 2005, the 2011 Republic Day chief guest visit by SBY and the 2023 India ASEAN joint statement on maritime cooperation. Indonesia, which led the enunciation of the ASEAN outlook on the Indo Pacific in 2019, is now associated with the Indo-Pacific Oceans Initiative (IPOI) of India.[8]

Despite challenges, the India-Indonesia relationship remains robust, characterised by mutual interests and a shared vision for regional stability and development. As both nations navigate their respective domestic and international landscapes, their partnership continues to play a vital role in the broader Indo-Pacific context.

The China Factor and Growing Islamic Influence

The second term of President Joko Widodo, popularly known as Jokowi, has seen a nuanced shift in Indonesia's domestic and foreign policies, significantly impacting the India-Indonesia relationship. One of the critical factors has been the growing Islamic influence on Jokowi's policies. Facing massive public protests led by radical Muslim groups beyond the traditional Nahdlatul Ulama and Muhammadiyah, Jokowi had to navigate these challenges with caution. To address these concerns, he nominated a prominent Muslim cleric as his vice president in his second term, replacing the more charismatic Jusuf Kalla. This move was aimed at appeasing the radical factions and stabilising the political climate.

The COVID-19 pandemic added another layer of complexity to this scenario. The Tablighi Jamaat incident, where many Indonesians were caught in the mass gathering case, led to prolonged diplomatic and domestic challenges. The slow resolution of this issue resulted in significant domestic unrest and protests outside the Indian Embassy, a level of discontent not seen since the protests at the Indian embassy during the Asian Games of 1962.

There are manifestations of new positions being taken by the Indonesian government. The position of Indonesia vis-a-vis the Organisation of Islamic Cooperation (OIC) and Palestine is one such aspect. The intra-ASEAN focus on the Rohingya issue in Myanmar is another. The rather quiet response to China's treatment of the Uighurs and the more vocal reaction to incidents in India show some aspects that need scrutiny.[9]

Despite these challenges, the period saw numerous ministerial and official meetings between India and Indonesia, both bilaterally and within the context of ASEAN, the East Asia Summit (EAS), and the ASEAN Regional Forum (ARF). While these fora provided ample opportunities for dialogue, the implementation of agreed-upon agendas has often lagged.

Indian companies frequently find the Indonesian market challenging, often lacking the patience required to navigate the local cultural and economic landscape. This challenge extends to political engagement, where deeper and more sustained efforts are needed to foster meaningful partnerships. While parliamentary exchanges offer potential, there is a clear need for more robust engagement at the civil society level. Think tanks, newspaper editors and student exchanges can provide significant value but often remain sporadic and embassy-driven rather than institutionally anchored.

Promising Initiatives and Future Directions

Some initiatives have shown promise, particularly the interfaith dialogues facilitated either by the Minister of State for External Affairs[10] or the National Security Advisor.[11] The "India–Indonesia Economic and Financial Dialogue" announced around the G20 meeting in 2023, the Energy and Trade Forums all exist. To be impactful, these require regular scheduling and the active involvement of the private sector and civil society organisations. Institutionalising these efforts can provide a more consistent and meaningful platform for bilateral cooperation.

Conclusion

The evolving dynamics of India-Indonesia relations during Jokowi's tenure reflect a complex interplay of religious, economic and geopolitical factors. Addressing these challenges requires sustained and multifaceted engagement, leveraging both formal diplomatic channels and grassroots civil society initiatives. As both nations navigate these complexities, a balanced and proactive approach will be crucial to n strengthening their partnership.

India and Indonesia are both getting used to the dynamics of a changing world. Indonesia is balancing its economic partnership with China with strategic autonomy towards others. India has serious problems with China, and is working with the Quad for resisting Chinese hegemony in the South China Sea and to provide public goods for the benefit of the Indo-Pacific region.

Both India and Indonesia are now part of the Indo-Pacific Economic Framework. India and Indonesia were successive G20 chairmen and have brought continuity to its agenda. However, Indonesia has been disinterested in joining BRICS. India would have been happier having Indonesia in it.

As India and Indonesia look on how to balance their respective strategic autonomies, they have the opportunity to cooperate more with each other. Over the last five years, the ministerial dialogues have picked up and the engagement is much more frequent. This needs to go to the level of the people, the youth, students and civil society.

India is providing a large number of tourists to Indonesia, but the flow of students and tourists from Indonesia to India is low. These trends need to be reversed.

With General Prabowo assuming the presidency, there is a likelihood of a more autonomous and balanced Indonesian regional policy in which India could play a role. The renegotiation of the AITIGA (ASEAN-India Trade in Goods Agreement) will also open more opportunities for regional value chains between India and Indonesia. Most importantly, the subjects covered in the Quad summits and the ASEAN Outlook on the Indo-Pacific provide a firm basis for expanding cooperation under the socio-cultural pillar of ASEAN between India and Indonesia.

Diplomatic engagements have succeeded over the years. It is now time for the people-to-people connect to keep pace with them.

NOTES

1 Gurjit Singh, Masala Bumbu: Enhancing the India-Indonesia Partnership, Berita Satu, 2015.

2 Ibid.

3 Important Milestones in the History of Indonesian Diplomacy, KEMLU, https://kemlu.go.id/portal/en/read/47/tentang_kami/important-milestones-in-

4 SD Muni, The Bandung Spirit: India and Indonesia in a Resurgent Asia, in Gurjit Singh ed Masala Bumbu: Enhancing the India-Indonesia Partnership, Berita Satu, 2015, pp. 50-55 Agreements signed during the State Visit of President of Indonesia, MEA, 25 January 2011, https://www.mea.gov.in/bilateral-documents.htm?dtl/3733/Agreements+signed+ during+ the+ State+Visit+of+President+of+Indonesia

5 Agreements signed during the State Visit of President of Indonesia, MEA, 25 January 2011, https://www.mea.gov.in/bilateral-documents.htm?dtl/3733/Agreements+signed+during+ the+ State+Visit+of+President+of+Indonesia

6 Gurjit Singh, The Foreign Policy Triad of Jokowi, *The Rising Asia Journal*, Vol. 1, Issue 1, Jan-April2021, https://www.rajraf.org/article/the-foreign-policy-triad-of-jokowi/1010

7 Gurjit Singh, The India ASEAN AOIP-IPOI cooperation, ORF,15 October 2022, https://www.orfonline.org/expert-speak/the-india-asean-aoip-ipoi-cooperation

8 Gurjit Singh, Islam and its role in Indonesia's foreign policy. ORF, 24 June 2020, https://www.orfonline.org/expert-speak/islam-role-indonesia-foreign-policy-68410

9 Dr. Temjenmeren Ao, India-Indonesia Interfaith Dialogue, ICWA. 26 September 2018. https://www.icwa.in/show_content.php?lang=1&level=3&ls_id=2527&lid=1878

10 India, Indonesia must jointly propagate moderate values of Islam: NSA Doval, Awaz The Voice, 30 November 2022, https://civilizationalvalues.org/media/2022/awaz_india-and-indonesia-must-collaborate-to-propagate-moderate-values-of-islam-nsa_11-30-22.pdf

4

Indonesia: Not a Distant Neighbour but a Sibling of India, an Indic Family Member

*Pulind Samant**

An analytical discussion is expected in this write up on India's relations with its immediate and distant neighbours, and the various factors influencing these relations, with a view to understanding whether the immediacy of physical proximity is what matters for India to help shape her foreign policy or otherwise.

India's Neighbours

Although the phraseology of immediate and distant neighbour may not have been used exactly and extensively in international relations scholarship, the word "neighbourhood" has been in vogue for some time, especially for elaborating challenges faced by India. In fact, the Government of India had used it in 2014 to pronounce its 'Neighbourhood First' policy and initiated a few symbolic activities, including sending invites to heads of all SAARC (South Asian Association for Regional Cooperation) states to be guests of honour at the swearing in ceremony of Prime Minister Narendra Modi in May of that year.

Although India had viewed the SAARC nations as her own neighbourhood in 2014, by November 2016, the scenario had changed after New Delhi decided to boycott the SAARC Conference in Islamabad, Pakistan, a move which was supported by three other SAARC member nations, namely Afghanistan, Bangladesh and Bhutan. Thereafter, India began eying another regional grouping – BIMSTEC (Bay of Bengal Initiative for Multi-Sector Technical and Economic Cooperation) – as potentially a promising one within her

*Pulind Samant is an independent researcher; who writes on civilisational and cultural issues.

neighbourhood, for furthering her own and the region's interests. India's Minister of External Affairs, Dr S. Jaishankar, soon after his appointment in 2019, had justified this move by underlining the fact that India saw "energy, mindset and possibility" in BIMSTEC. He simultaneously also dismissed the possibility of continuing with SAARC, blaming it for multiple and known problems of history and identity[1] associated with it. By virtue of that intentional review, India, reconstructed the definition of its own neighbourhood by default. The very fact that Myanmar was a BIMSTEC member as opposed to it being only an observer in the SAARC since 2008 along with Thailand, establishes that observation. India, thus, had effectively included a part of Southeast Asia in its own neighbourhood.

Changing Scenario

Moving a step further in 2020, Prime Minister Modi spoke about the 'extended neighbourhood' of India, during his address to the nation on the occasion of India's 74th Independence Day, wherein he clarified and asserted: "Today, neighbours are not only those with whom we share geographical boundaries, but also those with whom our hearts meet." Although he did not define the term explicitly, he had addressed the ASEAN (Association of South East Asian Nations) as India's maritime neighbours[2]. Prime Minister Modi's stress upon India's age-old religious and cultural ties with those nations was obviously made with a view to publicly embracing them as friends, even though their distance geographically may not be perceived as being in India's immediate neighbourhood, with the exception of Myanmar, and more particularly with regard to the segregation of the world's geography in certain straightjackets as done by the colonial powers, just as how the Indian subcontinent was termed as South Asia. Secondly, in terms of sheer physical distance, the shortest distance between India (its south-western Lakshadweep Islands) and Maldives (its north-eastern tip, Kulhudhuffushi), which is considered India's neighbour, is 413 kilometres. In comparison, the distance between India (Indira Point of the Nicobar Islands) and Indonesia (Sabang, the north-western tip of Sumatra province), is only 193 kilometers. In view of this comparative position of physical distances from Maldives to India in the west, and from India to Indonesia in the east, the claim, if any, for India's neighbourhood should actually tilt in favour of Indonesia than Maldives.

Meeting of Hearts

Going by the guideline of meeting of hearts as enunciated by Prime Minister Modi, in the context of identifying neighbours, Indonesia is seen as fitting in well with the extended neighbourhood as India's maritime neighbour and as an ASEAN founder member. India and Indonesia have had links with each other since beyond the Common Era, and in international relations terminology, almost two millennia before both emerged as modern nation states after the colonial period. Their relations can be described as civilisational, encompassing aspects of culture, ethnicity and religion. The Indonesian Archipelago has been historically referred to as the Indian Archipelago, East Indies, etc. by historians of the 19th and 20th centuries[3]. While ancient Indians referred collectively and generally to the whole of Southeast Asia (including Indonesia, but possibly excluding parts of the Philippines), as Suvarnabhumi (Sanskrit for 'Land of Gold'[4]), many European historians referred to the same geography as Further India[5], Greater India[6], or Farther India[7].

The Southeast Asia region, more identified by the ASEAN regional grouping tag, is divided into two sub-regions, namely, mainland and maritime, consisting of five each of the total of ten member states of ASEAN. While Cambodia is identified by scholars as the most India-influenced territory from within the mainland sub-regional lot[8], that identification in the maritime sub-region can be associated with Indonesia. While indigenous Indonesians have traditionally referred to the land of their ancestors only as Nusantara (Bahasa Indonesia for 'archipelago'), the name Indonesia, meaning 'Islands of India' in Greek, had been coined by European visitors and popularised by German ethnologist Adolf Bastian through his writings. The same name was accepted and used by Indonesian nationalist groups during their struggle for independence from the Dutch and assigned it to the modern nation-state post-independence[9].

Indic Background of Indonesia

Having noted Indonesia's etymological connection with India and its inclusion by historians in the 'Greater India' of their perception, it would be necessary to reveal background details that justify this perception. Before the advent of Islam in Indonesia in the 12th century, and even until it gained strength enough to become the dominant power there in the early part of the 16th century

C.E., Indonesia was known for its mighty and prosperous Buddhist and Hindu kingdoms of Sri-Vijaya (c. 4th–11th century C.E.), Shailendra (c. 7th–13th century C.E.) and Majapahit (13th–16th century C.E.) respectively. Sri-Vijaya, first independently and later as a part of the Shailendra Empire, regulated and prospered from the international trade flowing through the Malacca Straits under its control, being based in eastern Sumatra. While the Malaysian Peninsula-based Shailendras were the strongest power of their times in Southeast Asia, including a large part of Indonesia, the same status was enjoyed by the Majapahit later. Before the beginning of Dutch colonial rule in Indonesia, i.e., three centuries before common Indonesians started viewing their archipelago as their nation, the Majapahit had politically united more or less the same territory as one state, having vassal states close by. This historical fact being well known to Indonesians, especially the ruling class among them, it was a matter of pride and served as a rallying point during their struggle for independence against the Dutch. Sukarno, the first president of independent Indonesia, used to hang the Majapahit Empire map in his office, as the symbol of pride.

The Hindu faith is considered to have travelled from India to Indonesia and got established there in the early centuries of the Common Era, the evidence of which is found in inscriptions dated tentatively between the 1st and 4th century CE. The Buddhist faith, also from India, is considered to have spread there in the 5th century CE, though it had reached mainland Southeast Asia before the Common Era, during Mauryan Emperor Ashoka's reign. The archipelago's entire socio-cultural life was modeled on India, including the arts, language, literature, architecture, statecraft, etc., over centuries, a process which was termed by renowned French historian, George Coedes (1886-1969), as 'Indianisation'. Even Islam, which is Indonesia's dominant religion today, first surfaced in western Sumatra, via India, though later it entered elsewhere, especially in Java, through other channels emanating from within the Southeast Asian region. The credit for the process of Indianisation goes to the several Indians who visited the archipelago as adventurous sailors, enterprising traders, fortune-seeking princes, monks and priests, who had been invited there for religious purposes, including for solemnising the coronations of indigenous kings who were keen on benchmarking the Indian practice. While many of them stayed there for short durations, driven by various pursuits of their own, some of them settled there permanently, marrying locally and expanding their families. According to a local legend, one of the most prominent Indian names among such settlers is Sage Agastya, who is known and revered as Bhatara Guru by the local populace, especially by the people of Java. Bhatara stems from the Sanskrit word "Bhattara", with both meaning, "revered or venerable."[10]

Indic sources for information pertaining to civilisational affinity between India and Indonesia include Hindu texts like Valmiki's Ramayana, Kshemendra's Ramayana-Manjari, Harivamsha, a number of Puranas, namely, Vayu, Vishnu, Garuda, Markandeya, Vamana, Matsya and Brahmanda; Buddhist literature of Jataka, Milinda-panha and Niddesa, and a collection of stories like the Katha-Sarit Sagara. The Hindu sources mainly locate places in Indonesia like Java and Sumatra, along with places in the adjoining geography of Peninsular Malaysia; others mainly render stories of travels of Indians there, and related or incidental information. All of them, however, collectively corroborate the history of socio-cultural interaction of India with Suvarna-Bhumi, that is, today's Southeast Asia; many of them locate Suvarna-dvipa and Yava-dvipa, which have been identified with today's Sumatra and Java, by modern historians. The most interesting of the above facts emerges from the Valmiki Ramayana – when Rama was on the mission to locate Sita post her abduction by Ravana, the monkey-king in exile, Sugriva, sends out messengers in all directions for the purpose; one of those places had included Yava-dvipa (Java). This underlines the knowledge of the then Indians, Rama and his colleagues, of the existence of Java and its vicinity, and their perception about those territories as being in their neighbourhood.

The scholarly work of historians, both Indian and others, has discovered Indic influence in the languages of Indonesia, especially Javanese, as also on its literature. Old Javanese, the known oldest language of the Hindu-Javanese society was heavily influenced by Sanskrit[11]. Its literary version, called Kawi, was even more infused with Sanskrit vocabulary. Several notable literary works like the Ramayana, the Arjuna-Vivaha, the Bharat-yuddha (the Indonesian version of Mahabharata[12]) and the Brahmanda-Purana[13] were produced in Kawi. In fact, the national language of independent Indonesia is Bahasa Indonesia, where the word "Bahasa" is nothing but Bhasha (Sanskrit for language).

Bilateral Relations between Modern States of India and Indonesia

The above account proves Indonesia's civilisational status as a member of the Indic family, and thus, a sibling of India as stated in this paper's title. Now, whether this status has reflected modern Indonesia's brotherly political behaviour towards India remains to be seen. Such behaviour was visible when both were struggling for their independence from colonial rule. In the 'Asian Relations Conference' organised in New Delhi between March 23 and April 2, 1947, Jawaharlal Nehru announced the withdrawal of Indian troops from Indonesia who were fighting against Indonesian freedom-fighters on the orders of their British commanders, as Britain had sided with their fellow European colonialists, the Dutch[14]. But much before this official position was taken by India; Indian troops present in Indonesia were reportedly supplying arms occasionally, presumably out of brotherly feelings, to Indonesian freedom fighters secretly during the historic Battle of Surabaya in 1945[15]. Thereafter in 1948, India's pilot politician, Biju Patnaik, risked his life by rescuing Indonesian freedom struggle leaders Mohammed Hatta and Sultan Syahrir before Dutch colonial authorities could arrest them. They were flown to India on Prime Minister Nehru's instructions. Later in 1950, Sukarno, independent Indonesia's first President, was invited as the guest of honour to India's first Republic Day parade on January 26, 1950. When the Tsunami earthquake took place in December 2004, Indonesia was hit the hardest among the eleven affected nations, including India. The Indian Navy was the first foreign naval force to reach the Indonesian shores for rescue and relief operations. It launched 'Operation Gambhir' focusing on Indonesia, by deploying two warships there with 40 tons of relief aid, including three tons of medical relief supplies. One of those warships was converted into a 50-bed hospital ship, equipped with medical facilities like X-ray and ICU. Indian Naval groups were able to start those operations within 12 hours of the Tsunami's eruption. India was also among the first nations to provide assistance amounting to USD one million in relief supplies to Indonesia following the disaster[16]. During the COVID-19 virus, humanitarian assistance was done by both sides. While Indonesia sent 200 oxygen concentrators and 1400 oxygen cylinders to India, in May 2021, India reciprocated in kind in July 2021[17] by sending 300 oxygen concentrators and 100 metric tons of liquid medical oxygen under its 'Operation Samudra Setu' Scheme[18].

Indonesia has shown consistency in maintaining healthy bilateral relations with India, especially in the areas of defence and security. In May 2018, during the visit of Prime Minister Modi to Indonesia, a new Defence Cooperation Agreement was signed to reflect the elevation of relationship to a Comprehensive Strategic Partnership. Indonesia also emerged as India's second largest trading partner in Southeast Asia in Fiscal 2021-22[19].

Indonesia has extended its co-operation to India on important occasions at international fora. It opposed moves within the Organisation of Islamic Co-operation (OIC) during its annual meets, to issue strong statements on Kashmir[20]. Being the largest Muslim majority nation in the world, Indonesia presumably used its position within the OIC to facilitate an invitation to India to be the guest of honour at the OIC meeting in March 2019, hosted by the United Arab Emirates (UAE). Indonesia's Foreign Minister, Retno Marsudi, had then justified the invitation by underlining the ethos of pluralism and the value of democracy commonly shared between India and Indonesia, and their joint effort to strengthen co-operation to create peace and tolerance in the world[21]. She also asserted the commonality of goals between India and Indonesia in their respective Indo-Pacific strategies, in support of the position taken[22]. More recently, in 2020, Indonesia had refrained from commenting on India's decision to abrogate Article 370 of the Constitution, which revoked the Special Status granted to the state of Jammu and Kashmir, whereas its immediate neighbour, Malaysia, which shares religious, linguistic and ethnic ties with it, openly took a hostile position against India. Indonesia's position of not entertaining the Kashmir issue as a dispute of international relevance has been maintained. It can probably be seen as a continuing reciprocation of India's similar gesture in the past with regard to the southeastern island of Timor the eastern half of which eventually became independent East Timor in 2002 after an armed struggle with Indonesia. India not only refrained from commenting on the issue against Indonesia but also declined a proposal to join the United Nations Peacekeeping Force (UNPF) in that territory[23].

More importantly, Indonesia, in its capacity as a non-permanent member of the United Nations Security Council (UNSC), and also as the head of the Sanctions Committee on Counterterrorism within the UNSC, played a key role in declaring Pakistan-based Islamic terrorist Masood Azhar as a global terrorist in 2019. Indonesian Foreign Minister Marsudi then referred to the rise in the radical ideas as well acts of terror as being areas of common concern for both nations. She had also said that terrorism could not be justified under the pretext of religion[24], thus expressing solidarity with India.

Going by the construct of 'common goals in their respective Indo-Pacific strategies' and also under the 'shared vision of maritime co-operation in the Indo-Pacific' as identified during Prime Minister Modi's visit to Indonesia in May 2018, India has been working on developing its maiden deep-sea port in partnership with Indonesia, on the latter's Sabang Island, so as to have strategic access in the region, especially as a counter-balancing force[25]. Sabang is positioned at the mouth of the Malacca Straits and is considered a key global choke point. It is located around 90 nautical miles from India's Andaman and Nicobar Islands, which has been identified as "primary areas of interest" by the Indian Navy in the 'Indian Maritime Security Strategy' document[26]. These islands are uniquely positioned for India to undertake surveillance operations along the Straits of Malacca, falling between Indonesia's Sumatra and Peninsular Malaysia.

The world is aware about China's aggressive and unilateral marking of its own boundaries in the South China Sea (SCS), thereby restricting strategic and commercial movements by the affected littoral states of Southeast Asia. Indonesia is not a SCS claimant, but it has the experience of facing similar territorial skirmishes with China in the past, with regard to its northernmost island of Natuna Besar. It therefore started building a military base on that island in December 2018. This move has strategic and security relevance for India, in view of China's increasing presence of distant water fishing (DWF) vessels[27] and warships[28] in the Indian Ocean Region (IOR) on India's eastern flank. Any fortification such as at Natuna is a step in helping India to strengthen its own security and indirectly facilitating her emergence as a net security provider in the IOR region. This point was asserted by Prime Minister Modi at his UNSC address during India's month-long presidency in August 2021.

Conclusion

India and Indonesia share strong civilisational bonds built over a couple of thousand years. Both nations have asserted their values of pluralism and democracy as modern nation states and also demonstrated determined consistent growth post-independence. It is a cliché to say that you cannot choose your neighbours and to adjust your ways of cohabitation with them. India has been facing several issues of concern with its newly created 'immediate neighbours' post-partition, reflected in several ways, including in the bottlenecks experienced in the operation of the SAARC regional grouping. With that backdrop, the multifaceted co-operation and political understanding record of seemingly 'distant neighbour' Indonesia is commendable. The root cause of this apparent contrast can be understood simply analysing related history. Those immediate neighbours had attained their status by willingly separating not only their territories from India, but also severing their civilisational ties by giving primacy to religion over everything else and taking adversarial positions consequentially. Indonesia, on the other hand, though a Muslim majority demographically, has always cherished its Indic civilisational past and its lasting bond with India and other Indic families. This sense of being a member of the Indic family has apparently overwhelmed the sense of physical proximity or otherwise and also reflected the consistency of brotherly political behavior throughout.

Indonesia is most strategically located in the Indo-Pacific, possessing the largest territory, one of the strongest economies in the world and the biggest military power in Southeast Asia, a region considered central to the Indo-Pacific construct. Indonesia also is the headquarters of ASEAN, of which it is a founder member. Thus, it is in India's permanent interest to maintain and strengthen this bond, Indic as well as geo-strategic, with Indonesia, which is a fellow G20 member, from whom India assumed the group presidency last year.

NOTES

1. *The Economic Times*, 07 June 2019, p. 2.
2. "India has deepened ties with all countries in 'extended neighbourhood: PM Modi", *Times of India*, 15 August 2020, https://timesofindia.indiatimes.com/india/india-has-deepened-ties-with-all-countries-in-extended-neighbourhood-pm-modi/articleshow/77562855.cms
3. "Suvarnadvipa", S.R. Goyal in India's Interaction with Southeast Asia (Vol. 1, Pt. 3), G.C. Pande (Ed.), centre for Studies in Civilizations, New Delhi, 2006, p. 262.
4. Southeast Asia is India's El-Dorado, R.K. Dube, in India's Interaction with Southeast Asia (Vol. 1, Pt. 3), G.C. Pande (Ed.), Centre for Studies in Civilizations, New Delhi, 2006, p. 87.
5. Letters from the Far East, Charles Eliot, Edward Arnold, London, 1907, p. 47.
6. Civilization of the East (Vol. II), M. Rene Grousset, 1929 (quoted in Discovery of India, Jawaharlal Nehru, The John Day Co., New York, 1946, p. 201); Towards Angkor, H.G. Quaritch Wales, 1933 (quoted in Jawaharlal Nehru, op. cit., p. 203); Sumatra, Edwin M.

Loeb and Robert von Heine-Geldern, 1935 (quoted in South Indian Influences in the Far East, K.A.N. Sastri, Hind Kitabs Ltd., Bombay, 1949, pp. 114-115).

7. See The Indianized States of Southeast Asia, George Coedes and Susan B. Cowing and Walter Vella, Honolulu East-West Centre Press, 1968.
8. "Indian Cultural Heritage in Cambodia", B.R. Chatterjee in India's Contribution to World Thought and Culture, 1970, and The Making of Southeast Asia, George Coedes, 1966 (quoted in "Hinduism in Southeast Asia: Burma, Champa, Kambuja, Ceylon, Bali and Indonesia", V.C. Srivastava in India's Interaction with Southeast Asia (Vol. 1, Pt. 3), G.C. Pande (Ed.), Centre for Studies in Civilizations, New Delhi, 2006, pp. 636, 648.
9. Justus M. van der Kroef (1951). "*The Term Indonesia: Its Origin and Usage*". *Journal of the American Oriental Society*. 71 (3): 166–71. doi:10.2307/595186. JSTOR 595186.
10. Sanskrit-English Dictionary, V.S. Apte, Motilal Banarasidas Publishers Pvt Ltd., Delhi, 2017, p. 452.
11. This term has been used by a number of historians to indicate the socio-cultural composition of then Javanese society. See India and Java, B.R. Chatterjee, Prabasi Press, Calcutta, 1933; K.A.N. Sastri (op. cit.); N.J. Krom and F.D.K. Bosch as quoted in Historians of South-East Asia, D.G.E. Hall (Ed.), Oxford University Press, London, 1961; Some Contribution of India to the Ancient Civilizations of Indonesia and Malaysia, H.B. Sarkar, Punthi Pustak, Calcutta, 1970.
12. Indian Influence on the Literature of Java and Bali, H.B. Sarkar, Greater India Society, Calcutta, 1934.
13. "South-East Asia and the Indian Ocean in the Puranas", S.N. Roy in India's Interaction with Southeast Asia (Vol. 1, Pt. 3), G.C. Pande (Ed.), centre for Studies in Civilizations, New Delhi, 2006, pp. 143-158.
14. India's announcement in the Asian Relations Conference of 1947, https://en.wikipedia.org/wiki/Asian_Relations_Conference#:~:text=Organized%20by%20the%20Indian%20 Council, and%20presided%20by%20Sarojini%20Naidu. Retrieved on 6 February 2023.
15. Asia Reborn, Prasenjit K. Basu, Aleph Book Co., New Delhi, 2017, p. 417.
16. Press Release, Embassy of India, Jakarta, 24 December 2004. https://www.mea.gov.in/Portal/CountryNews/3398_Press_Release_-_Government_of_India_expresses_solidarity_with_the_Government_ and_ the_ people _of_ Indonesia_on_the_ solemn_ occasion_ of_ Indian_Ocean_Tsunami_Disaster_commemoration.pdf , retrieved on 6 February 2023.
17. "Indonesia Sends COVID-19 Pandemic Management Assistance to India", Office of Assistant to Deputy Cabinet Secretary for State Documents & Translation, 12 May 2021. https://setkab.go.id/en/indonesia-sends-covid-19-pandemic-management-assistance-to-india/ , retrieved on 6 February 2023.
18. Press Release, Embassy of India, Jakarta, 24 July 2021. https://www.indianembassyjakarta.gov.in/whats_new?id=eyJpdiI6IlpmN3BVU1dPSm5 CRkp3NWZ2 K0lnZ0E9PSIsInZhbHVlIjoicW ZLcjl3WEc5d1JFd1EwS0pWZDFMdz09IiwibWFjIjoiNWVmNDRkMzYw M GM1MDc1 NTJlYzY3 Y2NhMTdkODViZWMzYTc4MThiMjc2NGE0YWYzNmUxMjFhMmIzZTJjN mRkMCJ9#:~:text=Embassy%20of%20India%2C%20Jakarta&text=Ambassador%20of% 20India %20to%20 Indonesia,wave %20of%20COVID%2D19%20pandemic, retrieved on 6 february 2023.
19. India-Indonesia Bilateral Brief (Unclassified) as on 25 November 2022. https://www.mea.gov.in/Portal/ForeignRelation/Indonesia22nov.pdf retrieved on 7 February 2023.

20. *The Economic Times*, 25 February 2019, p. 2.
21. *The Economic Times*, 25 March 2019, p. 3.
22. Ibid.
23. India and Southeast Asia: The Security Cooperation, Lt. Gen. Yoginder Mohan Bammi (Retd.), New Delhi, Gyan Publishing House, 2006, p. 199.
24. *The Economic Times*, 25 March 2019, p. 3.
25. *The Economic Times*, 20 March 2019, p. 3.
26. "Andaman and Nicobar can lift India's Maritime Capacity", Harsh Pant and Sohini Bose, *Hindustan Times*, 14 January 2023, p. 12
27. "Spurt in China's DWF Vessels in High Seas on Radar of Indian Security Set-up", Dipanjan Roy Chaudhury, *The Economic Times*, 6 February 2023, p. 2.
28. Admiral Karambir Singh's statement at the Raisina Dialogue 2020, Hindustan Times, 16 January 2020, p. 8.
29. "India Asserts its 'Net Security Provider role; in the Indian Ocean Region", Anirban Bhaumik, Deccan Herald, 10 August 2021. https://www.deccanherald.com/india/india-asserts-its-net-security-provider-role-in-indian-ocean-1017935.html, retrieved on 6 February 2023.

5

India's Ancient Connections with Indonesia

*Saudiptendu Ray**

Around the 1st century CE, cultural practices from the Indian subcontinent, which included language, script, ideas, stories, religion, tradition and architecture, began reaching Indonesia. These ancient cultural connections between India and Indonesia were facilitated by phases of migration from different parts of India and a growing sea trade. Developments in sea navigation and construction of sturdy ships helped to establish trade links between distant lands spread across oceans. Indonesia emerged as an important mid-point for ancient sea route trade with India, China and West Asia because of its abundance of spices like cloves, mace and nutmeg, besides other raw materials.[1] The Straits of Indonesia were also strategically located along these ancient sea routes. Ancient Indonesian traders and sailors also developed their own seafaring culture and their ships started reaching not only the coastal areas of India, but also the Arabian Peninsula and Madagascar in the west.[2] These ancient sea trade routes between India and Indonesia were not only channels for exchange of high-end goods from different regions, but also served as conduits for an exchange of ideas, belief systems, religion, socio-cultural practices, and people.

Indic religious traditions like Sanatan Dharma (Hinduism) and Buddhism started interacting through indigenous traditions prevalent in the islands of Indonesia and the rest of Southeast Asia in the early centuries of the Common Era. Indian cultural practices assimilated with the local culture of Indonesia because of the active local acquiescence. Dr N. J. Krom, a Dutch historian who has extensively studied Hinduism in Java, stated that Hinduism in

*Saudiptendu Ray is a Research Associate, Vivekananda International Foundation.

Indonesia was allowed to permeate into local culture easily and subsequently allowed to influence virtually every aspect of local life.[3]

The percolation of cultural ideas from India to Indonesia was not the result of colonisation. Unlike the transfer of culture across the world by the Europeans in the 18th, 19th and early 20th centuries, political subjugation was not a tool used to force feed cultural traits in Indonesia. Dr Krom had clearly stated that Hinduism did not spread in Indonesia through the subjugation of the masses by the prevailing political authority.[4] Indian traders, scholars and priests who had settled in the port cities of Indonesia may have acted as catalysts in the transmission of Indian cultural ideas. This transmission was largely peaceful, unlike the European colonial version. However, this transmission of culture may have been bilateral in nature with Indonesians also selectively adopting certain Indian ideas and bringing them back to Indonesia.

The resources in Suvarnabhumi, or Suvarnadvipa[5] (present-day Insular Southeast Asia, which comprises the countries of Indonesia, Malaysia, Brunei, etc.), always attracted the attention of Indian sea traders. They, however, required the support of Indonesian chiefs and kings in order to carry on their economic activities in the region. To ensure this support, Indian traders also sent their representatives, mostly Brahmins and Buddhist monks, to the king's court[6] to serve as advisers and facilitate overseas trade.[7]

The improvements in navigation, particularly the construction of larger shipping vessels[8] and the effective use of monsoon winds, helped in developing an efficient trade link with Southeast Asia, especially with Indonesia. According to Ptolemy (2nd century CE Greek mathematician and astronomer), vessels sailed between the Port of Palur[9] (near the modern-day port of Gopalpur in Odisha) to the Malay Peninsula and beyond. The ancient Greco-Roman manuscript, Periplus (a document that lists ports and coastal landmarks), also mentions the existence of sea routes leading to Southeast Asia from three harbours located on the eastern coast of India. Beside these sea routes, India's cultural practices also reached Indonesia and Southeast Asia via the land routes through Eastern Bengal, Assam, Manipur and Burma.

The earliest textual evidence of Indonesia in India comes from Buddhist religious texts. *Milindapanha*, composed in the 1st century CE, to guide kings, mentions the island of Sumatra. Similarly, *Mahaniddesa*, a 3rd century CE

Pali text, mentions the island of Java.[10] We also find references to Java (referred to as *Yavadvipa*) in our revered text, the Ramayana. After Mother Sita was abducted by Ravana, Lord Rama took the assistance of Sugriva's army to search for her. Sugriva dispatched a section of his soldiers across the ocean to *Yavadvipa* in search of Mother Sita.[11]

The earliest physical evidence of India's material culture in Indonesia can be found in the excavated statues of Lord Buddha from different parts of Indonesia.[12] These include the discovery of a bronze statue of the Amravati Buddha, Dipangkara, found in 1921 at Sikendeng near the mouth of the Karama River in Sulawesi Island, dating back to the 2nd to 7th centuries CE[13], and the statue of Buddha from Palembang in Sumatra. Both statues were made in the Amaravati style that evolved in the region of Amaravati located between the lower valley of the rivers Krishna and Godavari in modern-day Andhra Pradesh from the 2nd century BCE to the end of the 3rd century CE.[14] The statue of Buddha from Palembang is made of granite, a type of stone not found in and around Palembang in Indonesia. It is possible that these Amaravati-style statues of Buddha might have been brought to Indonesia by Buddhist monks on a commercial ship sailing from India's peninsular south.[15] In recent excavations in Palembang, Sumatra, various artefacts like Indian pottery, gold-filigree beads and tin pendants were discovered, which affirms the exchange of goods within regional and long distance maritime networks.[16] In a small moated settlement in Kota Kapur in the Bangka Belitung Islands, archaeologists have discovered Hindu temples with statues of Lord Vishnu, Devi Mahishasurmardini and a Shiva Linga belonging to the 6th to 7th centuries CE.[17]

Vishnu statue excavated from Kota Kapur (Bangka)

Yupa inscription

Indonesian culture was further enriched with the arrival of Indic writing from India in the early centuries of the Common Era.[18] The vast majority of early inscriptions in Southeast Asia used the Brahmi script that evolved in Southern India. The earliest evidence of writing discovered in the Indonesian archipelago is from the seven Yupa inscriptions (sacrificial stone pillars), found in the area of Kutai, East Kalimantan (Borneo).[19] These Sanskrit inscriptions were written using the old Pallava script and date back to the Kutai Martadipura kingdom in the 4th-5th centuries CE.[20] The written script opened up the opportunity to spread human thoughts and ideas. Therefore, it can be said that the use of Sanskrit as a language by Indonesian natives played a major role in the acceptance of Indic religions in Indonesia.

In the present-day Bahasa language, Indonesia has many words derived from Sanskrit. The word '*Bahasa*' itself is derived from 'भाषा' (Bhasa), which in Sanskrit means language. The ancient stone inscriptions of the Srivijaya rulers (7th century CE) depict numerous Sanskrit words. In the course of the centuries, words originating from Sanskrit in Bahasa underwent natural changes in form and meaning. In some cases, some words have a completely different meaning than the root word in Sanskrit. This made it difficult to trace the Indian genesis of some of these words.[21] The pronunciation of some words originating from Sanskrit has evolved over thousands of years, and due to this long period of assimilation, these have entered the Indonesian vocabulary in such a way that they are no longer perceived as alien. The table below depicts a few examples of the words originating from Sanskrit.

Indonesian Word	*English Meaning*	*Sanskrit Root Word*	*English Meaning*
Aksara	Letter	अक्षर (Akṣara)	Letter
Bakti	Homage, loyalty	भक्ति (Bhakti)	Devotion
Cerita	Story	चारित (Cārita)	Story
Darma	Duty	धर्मः (Dharma)	Law, duty
Embara	Wandering	दिगम्बर (Digambara)	Wandering medicant
Garuda	Eagle	गरुड (Garuda)	Eagle
Harta	Property	अर्थ (Artha)	Object, property
Isteri	Wife	स्त्री (Strī)	Woman
Jiwa	Soul	जीव (Jiva)	Soul
Kepala	Head	कपाल (Kapala)	Skull
Lengkara	Ornament	अलंकार (Alankara)	Ornament
Manusia	Mankind	मनुष्य (Mānuṣya)	Mankind
Negara	State	नगर (Nagara)	City, state
Perdana	Prime Minister	प्रधान (Pradhāna)	Prime or principal
Raksasa	Giant, demon	राक्षस (Rākṣasa)	Giant malevolent beings
Satria	Knight, soldier	क्षत्रिय (Kṣatriya)	Warrior
Teruna	Young	तरुण (Taruṇa)	Young
Utara	North	उत्तर (Uttara)	North
Wijaya	Victory	विजय (Vijaya)	Victory
Yuda	Battle	युद्ध (Yuddha)	Battle

In the field of religion, animistic practices existed in Indonesia well before the advent of Hinduism and Buddhism.[22] These practices included a belief that spirits existed in all things on earth. It was considered that these spirits were capable of helping human beings. The indigenous people of Indonesia also had the concept of a creator (god) and other minor gods who fulfilled the daily needs of the people, like the prosperity of the tribe, fertility of cultivated soil, provider of food, fire and shelter, etc. They also worshipped and appeased the divine tricksters who brought disease and death.[23] Like the rest of the world, the early indigenous religions of Indonesia also had mediators between the gods and humans. These mediators were called priests and shamans.[24] The local chiefs were also very powerful and, in some cases, were worshipped even after their deaths. Therefore, before the advent of Indic Dharmas, religious beliefs in Indonesia were quite complex.

Some native religious practices in Indonesia were quite similar to Hindu and Buddhist religious practices. Indonesian natives might have regarded Hindu priests and Buddhist monks as being similar to their priests, shamans and medicine men, but with minor differences. Therefore, this religious and cultural transition did not bring any significant change in the lifestyle of natives.[25] This transition from indigenous beliefs to Hinduism and Buddhism was further aided by the fact that the locals placed Hindu priests and Buddhist monks on a higher pedestal than the indigenous Shamans because of the presence of written religious literature.[26]

The Hindu priests and Buddhist monks found a firm footing in the royal courts. They were invited to be part of the courts by local chiefs and kings. One such example is Gunavarman, a Kashmiri Buddhist scholar. He came to Indonesia in the early 5th century CE and became an adviser in the court of King Vadhaka of Java.[27] Upon Gunavarman's advice, the Javanese king waged a war and emerged victorious.[28] Gunavarman's prestige rose across the region and helped in promoting Buddhism at the royal court of Java. In most cases, whenever these types of Indian priests and monks became part of a particular royal household, the entire court started following the new religion propagated by them.

Indic religions provided powerful local kings and chiefs wider scope for their operations. Deities of Hinduism and Buddhism, having no local habitation, served the purpose of transcending the powers of all local gods. It allowed kings and chiefs to claim people and territories beyond their immediate surroundings and outside their own lineage.[29] For example, the Maharajahs of Srivijaya (7th century CE to 10th century CE) exercised their sovereignty over local chiefs and nobles of the island of Sumatra, the Malay Peninsula and the surrounding smaller islands on the straits by using symbols and attributes from Hindu and Buddhist iconography. To demonstrate their political authority, Indonesian sovereigns used titles like *Maharajah* and *Chakravartin*. Local Hindu kings from Java also attached the suffix *varman* to their names as tacit acknowledgement of their practice of Hinduism.[30]

Hinduism and Buddhism flourished almost at the same time in Indonesia. They not only co-existed, but were also so closely associated with each other that it was very difficult to distinguish their respective influences on Indonesian society. Tolerance and non-assertiveness were central to both religions. In Central Java, Hindu and Buddhist temples were built simultaneously between the 8th and 12th centuries, like Prambanan, Borobudur, Sewu, Barong Temple and the Candi Ijo. Prambanan, a temple dedicated to Trimurti (Brahma, Vishnu and Shiva), also had sculptures depicting the Bodhisattvas.[31] The Shailendra dynasty of Central Java followed Buddhism in the 8th century CE but maintained cordial relationships with the Shivaite King Sanjaya.[32] The synergy between Hinduism, Buddhism and native Indonesian belief systems formed Indonesian conceptions of kingship.

The amalgamation of Hinduism and indigenous local traditions also resulted in the emergence of the Devaraja order in Java. Under this religious order, the king is divine, or the human manifestation of God on earth. It enabled the monarch to claim divine authority and ensure his political legitimacy and control over the social order, the economy and religious aspects. The Devaraja order evolved from the Indian concept of Chakravartin, or the ideal universal ruler. Once the king's authority is established, he usually builds a sanctuary atop a mountain, or an artificial mound. At the top of the mound, a lingam is installed, symbolising the fiery essence and energy of Lord Shiva. The Lingam also represents the power of the king. The first records of this practice in Java are found in the Canggal Inscription dated 732 CE and the Dinaya Inscription dated 760 CE.[33] The Canggal Inscription records the installation of a Linga by King Sanjaya to consecrate a new Mataram Dynasty.[34]

The statue of Harihara, the deified portrayal of Emperor Raden Wijaya from the Majapahit Empire

The Yupa Inscriptions from Kutai, Borneo, provide the earliest evidence of a kingdom that was deeply inspired

Yupa Inscription mentioning the name of King Kundunga

by Indian culture. These Yupa Inscriptions were commissioned by King Mulavarman[35] of the **Kutai Martadipura Kingdom** in East Borneo (Kalimantan). The inscriptions mention the names of Kudungga, the founder of the kingdom, and his son Aswawarman. The Kutai Martadipura Kingdom was a Hindu kingdom, and rulers of the dynasty after Kudungga started adding 'Varman' as a suffix. King Mulavarman also performed the Ashwamedh Yagya in order to extend his political control over the island.[36] Aside from the inscriptions already mentioned, the Kutai region has also yielded some Brahminic and Buddhist sculptures as well.

The discovery of the Tarumanagara Inscriptions in West Java provides the earliest traces of a Hindu kingdom in Java.[37] This kingdom was called the **Tarumanagara Kingdom.** Most of the Tarumanagara Inscriptions were produced under King Purnawarman in the 5th century CE.[38] Some of these inscriptions talk about King Purnawarman's association with Lord Vishnu and various Brahminic rituals.[39] The Cidanghiang Inscription in Banten province in West Java mentions that King Purnawarman used the title Vikranta to associate himself with Lord Vishnu.[40] Vikranta was an appellation of Lord Vishnu, the conqueror of the three worlds. The worship of Lord Vishnu was prevalent in this period in Java. A fragment of Lord Vishnu was also discovered at the Batujaya Archaeological site in West Java.[41]

The cultural impact of Sanskrit and Hinduism in the Tarumanagara

Kingdom is also visible in the Ciaruteun Inscription discovered on the riverbed of the Ciaruteun River in West Java.[42] The Ciaruteun Inscription was written in Sanskrit using the Vengi Script of the Pallava period in Southern India. The Ciaruteun Inscription is written in the form of a Sanskrit sloka and depicts the foot prints of King Purnawarman. The foot prints have the lotus mark on them, which is considered an auspicious *lakshana* (mark) in Hinduism. Lotus marks on foot prints were also associated with Lord Vishnu. Another rock inscription in Merbabu Mountain in Central Java compares a local river to the Indian Ganges.[43]

The **Srivijaya Empire** became an important maritime power in Sumatra in the 7th century CE. It had control over the crucial straits on lucrative sea trade routes, namely the Strait of Malacca and the Sunda Strait. This enabled them to control trade taking place in the region. The Srivijaya Empire also emerged as an important centre for Buddhist studies. According to the Chinese Buddhist pilgrim, Yijing (635-713 CE), Buddhism was extensively researched by Buddhist monks in Srivijaya, and their way of life and discipline were exactly like those of the monks in *Madhyadesa* (India).[44] The rock edicts of the Srivijaya rulers were carved in the Old Malay language (an archaic version of Bahasa Indonesia) and written in Pallava script.[45] The Kedukan Bukit

Ciaruteun inscription

Inscription (dated 683 CE) discovered on the banks of the Tatang River is considered the oldest surviving specimen of the archaic Malay language written in Pallava script.[46] This practice of writing an Indonesian language with an Indian script depicts the confluence of cultures.

Kedukan Bukit inscription

The **Mataram Kingdom** flourished between the 8th and 11th centuries in Central Java and later in East Java. It originated from two different interrelated lineages of rulers, the Sanjaya dynasty, who were Shaivite, and the Shailendra dynasty, which followed Mahayana Buddhism. There are several inscriptions discovered in Central Java, produced under the Sanjaya rulers, that talk about Lord Shiva, like the Sojomerto Inscription, the Canggal Inscription and Shivagrha Inscription. On the other hand, the Shailendra rulers promoted Buddhism in Java and constructed the magnificent stupa at Borobudur. The assimilation of Hinduism and Buddhism impacted Javanese art and architecture. Under the Matarams, Javanese art and architecture reached its peak between the 8th and 9th centuries. This golden period saw the construction of numerous temples like the Sewu, Borobudur, Prambanan, Mendut, Plaosan and Kalasan in Central Java in a comparatively short stretch of time. The Javanese and Indic (Buddhist and Hindu) ideas associated with political power and spirituality, and competed as well as intermingled under the Mataram rulers, forming a dynamic political and religious atmosphere.[47]

A relief depicting Gandavyuha story from Borobudur

Indian temple architectural styles significantly influenced ancient Indonesian architecture, and the Borobudur Stupa is a prime example of this cultural confluence. The Borobudur Stupa has a pyramid-like shape with stepped terraces. The Stupa walls are decorated with intricate stone carvings and bas-reliefs. These stone carvings narrate stories from Buddhism and the Jataka tales. One such story on the walls of Borobudur is the story from the Gandavyuha Sutra, which originated from India. The decorative panels on the Borobudur are embellished with carved motifs like lotus, geometric patterns and mythical creatures like Vyala or Yali.[48] These motifs from Borobudur resemble carvings that appear on the Konark temple and other medieval temples across eastern India. Other Central Javanese temples that elucidate these remarkable similarities between Javanese and Indian architectural styles can be seen at Prambanan, the Sewu temple and the temples of the Dieng Plateau. The temples from East Java, like the Penataran temple, reflect more indigenous architectural features than the temples in Central Java.

The Ramayana and Mahabharata seeped into Indonesian culture as well as literature between the 1st and 6th centuries CE. Before discussing the importance of these Indian epics in Indonesian literature, it is important to note that even before the Ramayana physically reached Indonesian shores in the aforementioned time period, we find references to islands of Indonesia like Java (Yavadvipa) in the Ramayana.[49] Both of these Indian epics were embraced by the Indonesian people and started impacting the Indonesian performing arts. Wayang Kulit, which is a type of shadow puppetry and various other traditional dance forms, started narrating the stories from the Ramayana and Mahabharata.

Prambanan Temple

In Indonesia, there are several adaptations of the Ramayana, like the old Javanese Kakawin Ramayana and the Balinese Ramakavaca. The Kakawin Ramayana from Java is one of the many Ramayanas written outside the Indian subcontinent. The Kakawin Ramayana was composed under the reign of Maharaja Balitung of the Mataram Kingdom in Central Java around the 9th century CE.[50] It was written in the form of Javanese poetry, known as Kakawin. The Hindu temple at Prambanan features stone carvings depicting scenes from the Kakawin Ramayana. The author of the Kakawin Ramayana remains unknown and it is likely that it was composed over centuries and across generations.[51]

Panataran temple Ramayana Relief depicting Monkey god

The Balinese Ramakavaca evolved out of the Kakawin Ramayana when the latter crossed the Bali Strait and reached Bali. The Balinese script used to write the Ramakavaca has its roots in the ancient Indian Brahmi script. The Ramayan has remained significant to Balinese culture in the modern period. This is evident from the fact that a dance form, Kecak, was created in the early 20th century to perform scenes from the Ramayana. Kecak dancers enact scenes

Prambanan relief depicting Ravana kidnapping Sita

from the Ramayana, playing the roles of Rama, Sita, Lakshmana, Hanuman, Ravana and other characters amidst the constant percussive monkey-like chant of "*chak.*"

In Indonesia, the epic 18-day war fought at Kurukshetra is referred to as Bharatayuddha, which is also the Javanese translation of Mahabharata. This Indian epic was translated into old Javanese under the reign of Maharaja Isyana Dharmawangsa of the Mataram Kingdom.[52] According to Javanese traditions, the epic battle was fought in Dieng Plateau, near Banjarnegera in Central Java. The Dieng Plateau also has multiple small Hindu temples like the Arjuna Temple, the Srikandi Temple, the Bima Temple and the Gatotkaca temple, all built between the 7th and 8th centuries.

Arjuna temple in Dieng Plateau

Indo-Indonesian ancient relations demonstrate a metaphorical bridge through which both countries have exchanged culture over the millennia. The long-distance maritime trade provided Indic religions with a physical platform they needed to cross the choppy seas. The assimilation of Indic religions with the indigenous belief system in Indonesia created a culture that was unique to the archipelago. It left a permanent impact on modern Indonesian society. As far as material culture is concerned, the amalgamation of ancient Indian architectural style with Indonesian artistry resulted in the construction of ancient marvels like the Borobudur Temple, the Prambanan Temple and the temples of the Dieng Plateau. Therefore, the cultural interactions between India and Indonesia forged a lasting bond between these two ancient civilisations.

NOTES

1 Guy, John. *Lost Kingdoms: Hindu-Buddhist Sculpture of Early Southeast Asia*, Yale University Press, p. 113.

2 Brown, Colin. 2003. *A short history of Indonesia*, Allen & Unwin, p. 13.

3 Mohd. Zariat Abdul Rani. (2010). *The History of Hinduism and Islam in Indonesia: A Review on Western Perspective,* Makara Human Behaviour Studies in Asia, Volume 14, Article 6.

4 Mohd. Zariat Abdul Rani. (2010). *The History of Hinduism and Islam in Indonesia: A Review on Western Perspective*, Makara Human Behaviour Studies in Asia, Vol. 14, Article 6.

5 Majumdar, R. C. (1937). *Ancient Indian Colonies in the Far East*, Vol. II, *Suvarnadvipa*, Calcutta, Modern Publishing Syndicate, pp. 37-47.

6 Suleiman, S. (1974). *Concise Ancient History of Indonesia*, Jakarta, pp. 10-12.

7 Suleiman, S. (1974). *Concise Ancient History of Indonesia*, Jakarta, p. 12.

8 Majumdar, R.C. (1955). *Ancient Indian colonisation in Southeast Asia*, Baroda, p. 17.

9 Patra, Benudhar. *Indian History Congress Proceedings,* Vol. 74 (2013), Ports and Port Towns of Early Odisha: Text, Archaeology and Identification, pp. 54-63.

10 Louis Charles Damais, "Le Bouddhisme en Indonesie," *Presenoe du Bouddhisme*, France-Asie, Saigon-Paris, 1959, pp. 813-824.

11 Kapur, Kamlesh. *Portraits of a Nation: History of Ancient India*, Sterling Publishers Private Limited, p. 465.

12 Roxas-Lim, Aurora. Buddhism in Early Southeast: A Contribution to the Study of Culture Change, Asian Studies, pp. 82.

13 Sue O'Connor, David Bulbeck, Juliet Meyer. *The Archaeology of Sulawesi: Current Research on the Pleistocene to the Historic Period*, Australian National University Press, 2018, p. 5.

14 Mahajan, V. D., (2016). *Ancient India*, S. Chand Publishing, pp. 294, 295.

15 Suleiman, S. (1974). *Concise Ancient History of Indonesia*, Jakarta, p. 10-11.

16 Guy, John. *Lost Kingdoms: Hindu-Buddhist Sculpture of Early Southeast Asia*, Yale University Press, p. 114.

17 Guy, John. *Lost Kingdoms: Hindu-Buddhist Sculpture of Early Southeast Asia*, Yale University Press, p. 114. Koestoro, Manguin, and Soeroso 1998; Manguin 2009b, pp. 440–41

18 Guy, John. *Lost Kingdoms: Hindu-Buddhist Sculpture of Early Southeast Asia*, Yale University Press, p. 53.

19 Susanti, Ninny. Script and Identity of Indonesia. *Malindo-Journal of Malaysian and Indonesian Studies*, Vol. 1(1), October 2019, 1-7

20 Vogel, J. *The Yupa Inscriptions*, pp. 167-232. William H. Frederick and Robert L. Worden, *Indonesia- a country study* (2011), Library of Congress, pp. 7-8.

21 Sanskrit Loan-Words in Indonesian: An annotated check-list of words from Sanskrit in Indonesian and Traditional Malay. Vol. 41 (1997), p. 1.

22 Suleiman, S. (1974). *Concise Ancient History of Indonesia*, Jakarta, p. 11.

23 Suleiman, S. (1974). *Concise Ancient History of Indonesia*, Jakarta, p. 12.

24 Suleiman, S. (1974). *Concise Ancient History of Indonesia*, Jakarta, p. 12.

25 Suleiman, S. (1974). *Concise Ancient History of Indonesia*, Jakarta, p. 11.

26 Suleiman, S. (1974). *Concise Ancient History of Indonesia*, Jakarta, p. 11.

27 Rao, A. Panduranga. *Proceedings of the Indian History Congress*, Vol. 46 (1985), p. 623.

28 Roxas-Lim, Aurora. Buddhism in Early Southeast: A Contribution to the Study of Culture Change, Asian Studies, p. 83.

29 Roxas-Lim, Aurora. Buddhism in Early Southeast: A Contribution to the Study of Culture Change, Asian Studies, pp. 86-87.

30 Mohd. Zariat Abdul Rani. (2010). *The History of Hinduism and Islam in Indonesia: A Review on Western Perspective*, Makara Human Behaviour Studies in Asia, Vol. 14, Article 6.

31 Roy E. Jordan. *In Praise of Prambanan.* Dutch Essays on the Loro Jonggrang Temple Complex, KITLV Press, p. 81.

32 Krom, N. J., *Hindoe-Javaansche Geschiedenis*, Gravenhage, 1931, p. 283.

33 Roxas-Lim, Aurora. Buddhism in Early Southeast: A Contribution to the Study of Culture Change, Asian Studies, p. 86.

34 M. Fic, Victor (2003). *From Majapahit and Sukuh to Megawati Sukarnoputri: Continuity and Change in Pluralism of Religion, Culture and Politics of Indonesia from the XV to the XXI Century.* Abhinav Publications, p. 91.

35 Vogel, J. *The Yupa Inscriptions*, pp. 167-232. B. R. Chatterjee, *India and Java* (Calcutta, 1933), II, Inscription, pp. 8-19.

36 Tony Whitten; Greg S. Henderson; Muslimin Mustafa (2012). *The Ecology of Sulawesi (The Ecology of Indonesia Series, Vol. IV)*. Tuttle Publishing, p. 76.

37 Basa, K. K. (1998). Indian writings on Early History and Archaeology of Southeast Asia: A Historiographical Analysis. *Journal of the Royal Asiatic Society*, series 3, vol 8, p. 401.

38 Coedes, George (1975). Walter F. Vella (ed.). Translated by Susan Brown Cowing. *The Indianized States of Southeast Asia,* Canberra, p. 53.

39 Mary Somers Heidhues (2000). *Southeast Asia: A Concise History*. London: Thames and Hudson, pp. 45-63.

40 Santiko, Hariani (December 2013). *The Vedic Religion in Nusantara*. Amerta Arkeologi, p. 146.

41 Santiko, Hariani (December 2013). *The Vedic Religion in Nusantara*. Amerta Arkeologi, p. 146.

42 Epigraphia Indica and Record of the Archaeological Survey of India, Vol. XXII (1933-34), p. 4-5.

43 Suleiman, S. (1974). *Concise Ancient History of Indonesia*, Jakarta, p. 15.

44 Suleiman, S. (1974). *Concise Ancient History of Indonesia*, Jakarta, p. 17. William H. Frederick and Robert L. Worden, *Indonesia- a country study* (2011), Library of Congress, p. 8.

45 William H. Frederick and Robert L. Worden, *Indonesia- a country study* (2011), Library of Congress, p. 8.

46 J. G. De Casparis (1978). *Indonesian Chronology*. BRILL Academic, pp. 15–24.

47 William H. Frederick & Robert L. Worden, *Indonesia- a country study* (2011), Library of Congress, pp. 9-10.

48 Dumarçay, Jacques (1991). *Borobudur*. Singapore: Oxford University Press, p. 452.

49 "Yavadvipa" is mentioned in India's earliest epic, the Ramayana. Kapur, Kamlesh, *Portraits of a Nation: History of Ancient India*, New Delhi, p. 465.

50 Santoso, Soewito. (1980).*Ramayana Kakawin*, Vol. 1, New Delhi, p. 17.

51 Santoso, Soewito. (1980). *Ramayana Kakawin*, Vol. 1, New Delhi, p. 17.

52 Creese, Creese, *Women of the Kakawin World: Marriage and Sexuality in the Indic Courts of Java and Bali*, 2004, p. 253.

6

Indonesia-India Trade in Brief (1979-2022)

*Akhmad Jayad**

Data in this paper is obtained from the World Integrated Trade Solution (WITS) website of the World Bank (wits.worldbank.org). The value of Indonesia and India export-import data based on Standard International Trade Classification (SITC) Revision 2 (1974) is in US dollars from 1979 to 2022.

The introduction gives an overview of trade between Indonesia and India. It presents a breakdown of products based on section classification (SITC 1 digit) consisting of ten items, i.e. 0 for food and live animals, chiefly for food; 1 for beverages and tobacco; 2 for crude materials, inedibles, except fuels; 3 for mineral fuels, lubricants and related materials; 4 for animal and vegetable oils, fats and waxes; 5 for chemicals and related products; 6 for manufactured goods classified chiefly by material; 7 for machinery and transport equipment and 8 for miscellaneous manufactured articles.

The section on discussion provides a detailed examination of products based on division classification (SITC 2 digits). Section 0 consists of ten divisions. Sections 1, 2 and 3 contain two, nine and four divisions respectively. Sections 4, 5, and 6 have three, nine and nine divisions respectively, while Sections 7 and 8 consist of and eight divisions respectively. Section 9 (commodities and transactions not classified elsewhere) is not presented due to its small data and minimum availability.

*Akhmad Jayad is an Associate Fellow, The Habibie Center.

Introduction

Trade between Indonesia and India has been on a significant growth path since 1993. Before 1993, i.e. between 1979 and 1992, exports from both countries for each product group was below USD 100 million, except in 1982, when India exported food and live animals worth USD 199 million.

Indonesia's Exports to India

In 2022, Indonesia's exports to India touched USD 10.7 billion, while India's exports to Indonesia were worth USD 2.2 billion for the same products (mineral fuels, lubricants and related materials). Indonesia's exports of these products increased over 400-fold between 1995 and 2022.

Figure 1

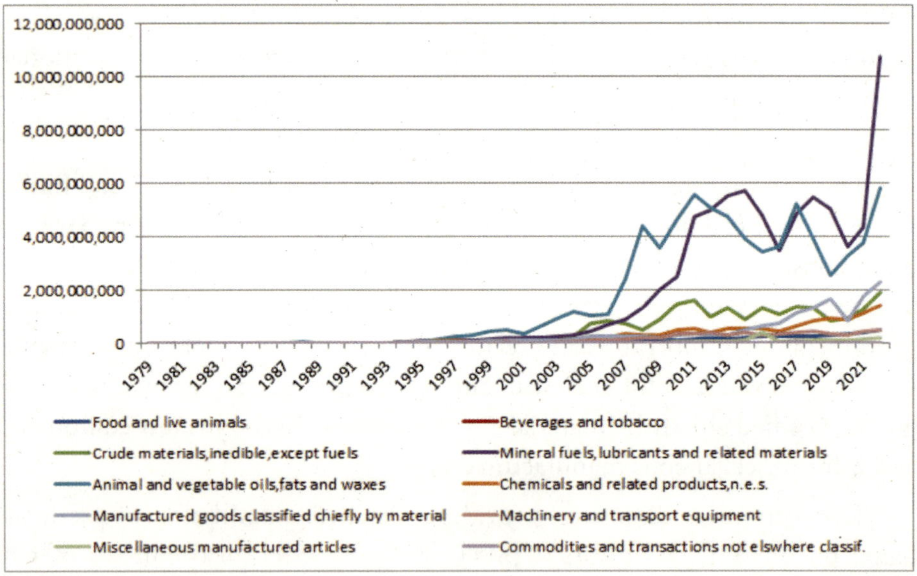

India's Export to Indonesia

Indonesia's other major exports to India in 2022 were animal and vegetable oils, fats and waxes, and manufactured goods classified chiefly by material. India's other significant exports to Indonesia on the other hand, were food and live animals, and machinery and transport equipment.

Figure 2

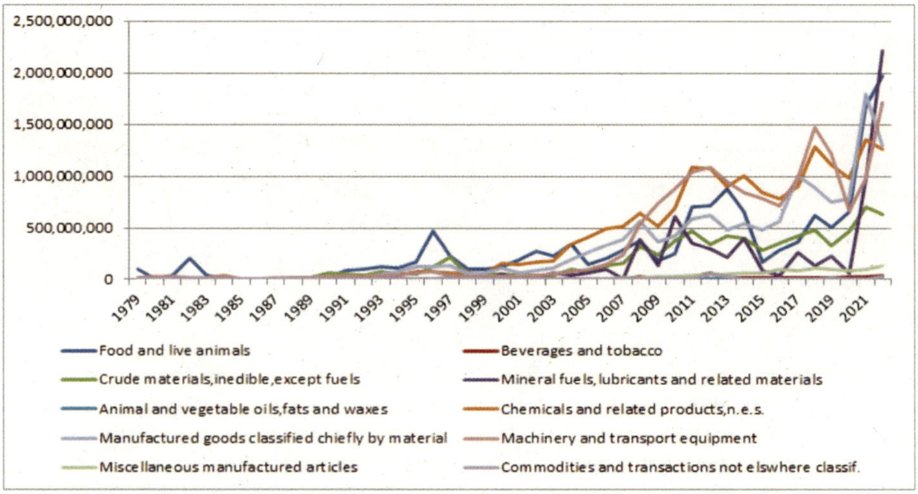

Discussion

Figure 3 to 11 illustrates Indonesia's net exports (export minus import) with India. A chart above the horizontal axis (positive value) indicates Indonesia having a trade surplus while India faces a trade deficit. On the contrary, the graph below the horizontal axis (negative value) shows Indonesia having a trade deficit, while India has a trade surplus.

Food and Live Animals

Figure 3 shows that in the food and live animals' section, Indonesia only experienced a surplus in two divisions, i.e., coffee, tea and cocoa, and spices, with a value of USD 343 million, and feeding stuff for animals worth USD 3 million in 2022. Indonesia maintained a surplus in vegetables and fruit products between 1991 and 2021, but then sharply dropped to a deficit of USD 147 million in 2022.

Among ten divisions in the food and live animal section, India had a surplus in seven divisions. Sequentially, the products were sugar, sugar preparations and honey (USD 844 million); Cereals and cereal preparations (USD 474 million); meat and meat preparations (USD 321); vegetables and fruits (USD 147 million); miscellaneous edible products and preparations (USD 25 million); dairy products and birds' eggs and fish, crustaceans, molluscs preparations thereof.

Figure 3

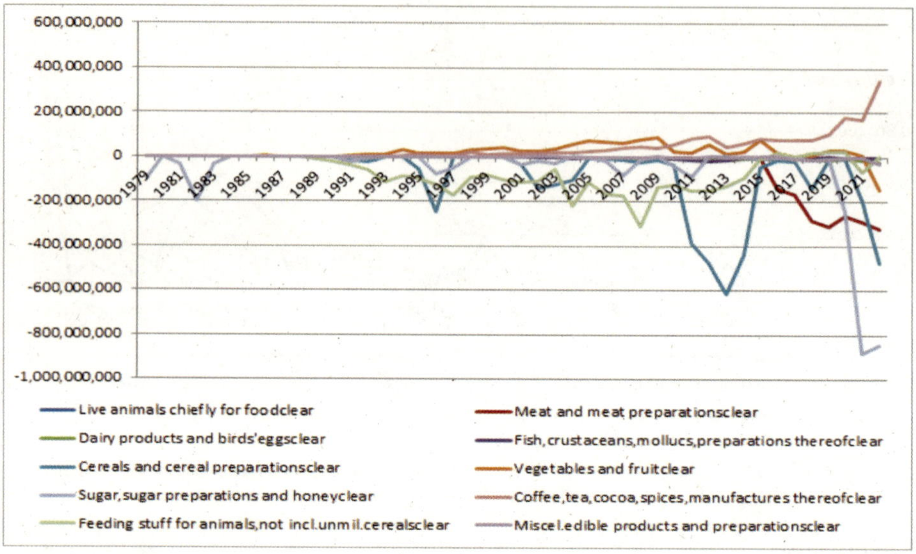

Beverages and Tobacco

Figure 4 shows the beverages and tobacco section, where Indonesia had a surplus in beverages products worth USD 301,000 in 2022. Since 1979, Indonesia's surplus has been at approximately that level, although there was a deficit of USD 70,000 in 2019.

Figure 4

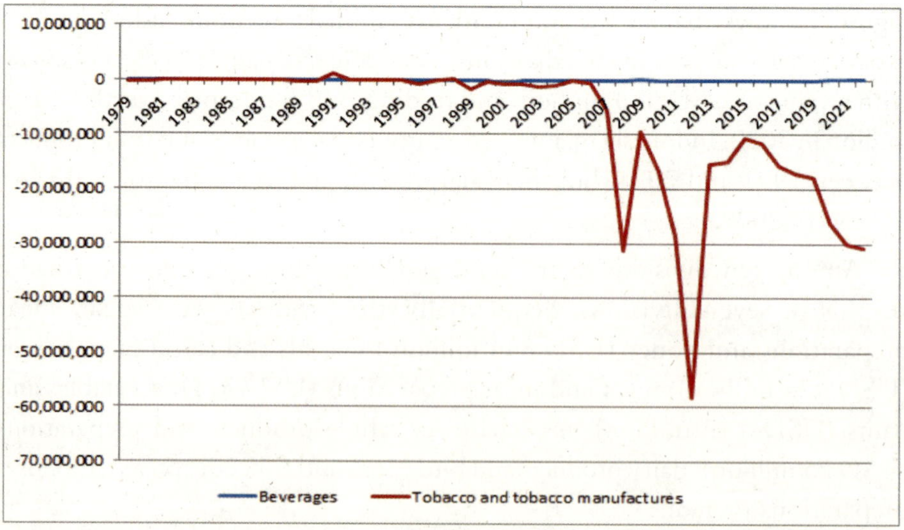

In contrast, India had a significant surplus in tobacco and tobacco manufactures products. India's largest surplus was in 2012, amounting to USD 58 million. Other large surpluses were in 2008 with USD 31 million and in 2022 with USD 30 million. India has dominated the bilateral tobacco trade, with Indonesia only achieving a USD one million in 1991.

Crude Materials, Inedible (Except Fuels)

Indonesia dominates India in bilateral trade on crude materials, inedibles, except fuels products, as shown in Figure 5. It has a surplus in six divisions, while India has a surplus only in three. Indonesia's largest surplus is from metalliferous ores and metal scrap products, reaching USD 1.2 billion in 2022.

The next five positive net exports of Indonesia respectively are pulp and waste paper; crude rubber (including synthetic and reclaimed); textile fibres (except wool tops) and their wastes and crude animal and vegetable materials. The smallest Indonesia surplus (USD 1.8 million) in this group is cork and wood products.

Figure 5

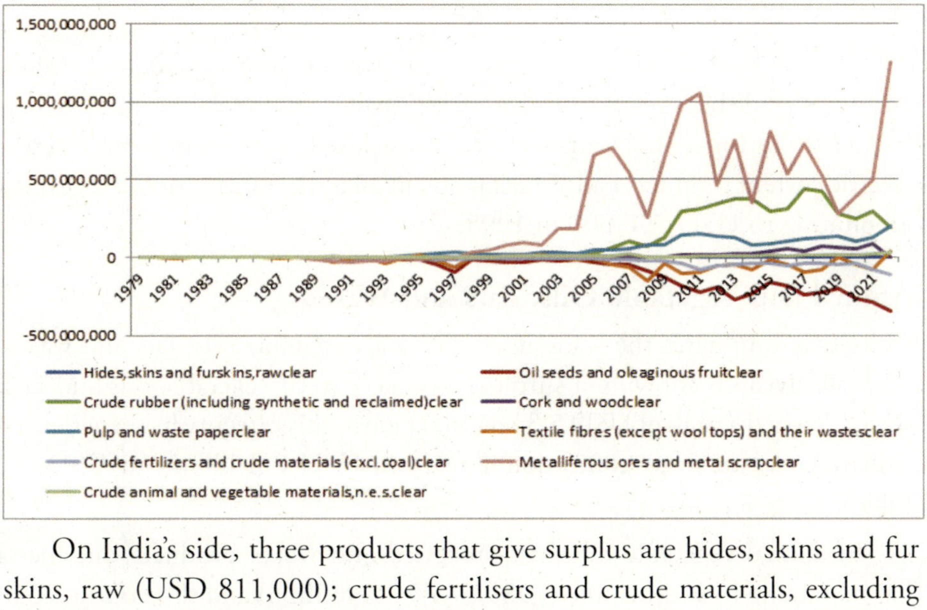

On India's side, three products that give surplus are hides, skins and fur skins, raw (USD 811,000); crude fertilisers and crude materials, excluding coal (USD 114 million) and oil seeds and oleaginous fruit that achieved its highest surplus at USD 341 million in 2022.

Mineral Fuels, Lubricants and Related Materials

In mineral fuels, lubricants and the related materials section, Indonesia experienced a significant surplus in coal, coke and briquette products (USD 10.6 billion). Conversely, India only enjoyed a slight surplus in petroleum, petroleum products and related materials at USD 2.1 billion.

Figure 6

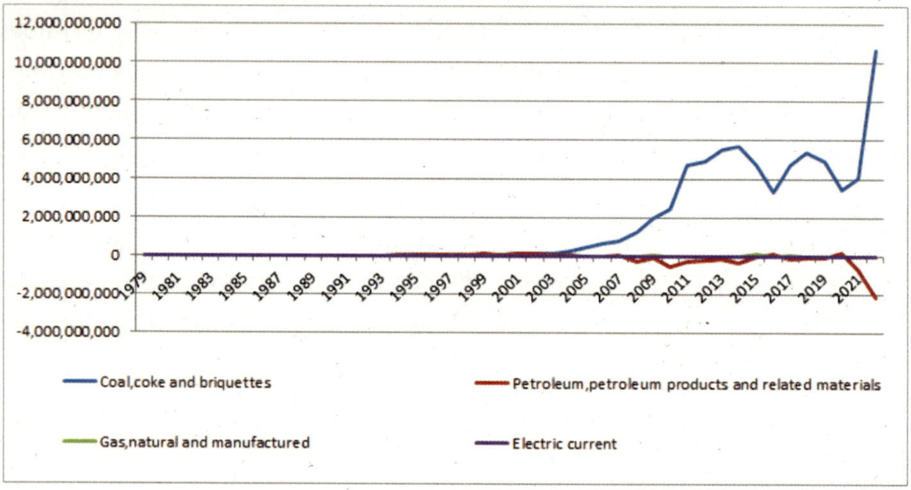

In the other two divisions — gas, natural and manufactured, and electric current— trade between the two countries is balanced. Indonesia's gas products had a surplus for several years with a value below USD 100 million, whereas electric current products had almost no bilateral trade, except for India's export amounting to USD 196,000 in 1995.

Animal and Vegetable Oils, Fats and Waxes

Indonesia dominates the trade in animal and vegetable oils, fats and waxes, with all divisions showing a surplus, especially fixed vegetable oils and fats, which reached a peak of USD 5.3 billion. Trade in this category has experienced a sharp increase since 2008, doubling from USD 2.3 billion to USD 4.2 billion. (Fig. 7)

In animal-vegetable oils-fats, processed and waxes products, Indonesia has maintained a surplus since 1984 (USD 2.6 million) and this continued to increase to USD 496 million in 2022. India only had a surplus in animal oils and fats products in 2022 at USD 34,000.

Figure 7

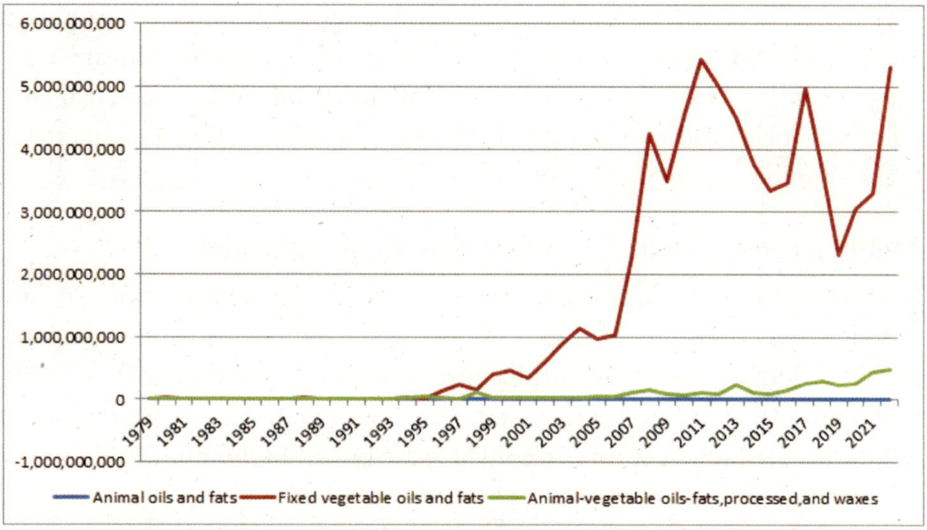

Chemicals and Related Products

The chemicals and related products section consists of nine divisions. Indonesia recorded a surplus in four divisions, while India had a surplus in five divisions. Indonesia's largest surplus was in manufactured fertilisers (USD 239 million), while India's largest surplus was in organic chemical products (USD 225 million).

Figure 8

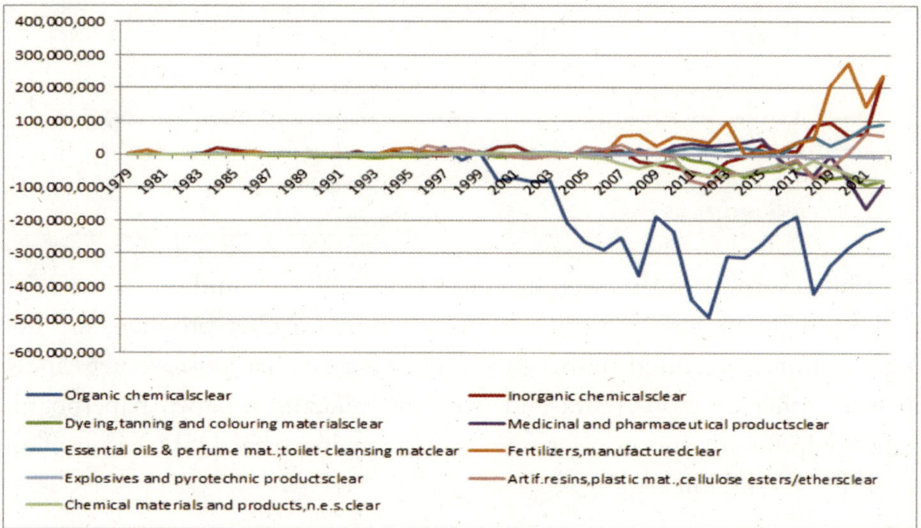

Indonesia's surplus with a similar value (ranging from USD 55 million to USD 95 million) is in artificial resins, plastic materials, cellulose esters/ethers; essential oils and perfume materials, and toilet-cleansing materials. Meanwhile, India's surplus is in dyeing, tanning and colouring materials; medicinal and pharmaceutical products, and chemical materials and products (ranging from USD 79 million to USD 93 million).

Manufactured Goods Classified Chiefly by Material

In the manufactured goods section, Indonesia and India's net exports are similar. Indonesia has a surplus in five divisions, while India has a surplus in four divisions. Indonesia's largest surplus is in iron and steel products (USD 670 million in 2022). These products were previously dominated by India since 1990 with the highest surplus recorded at USD 323 million in 2017.

Figure 9

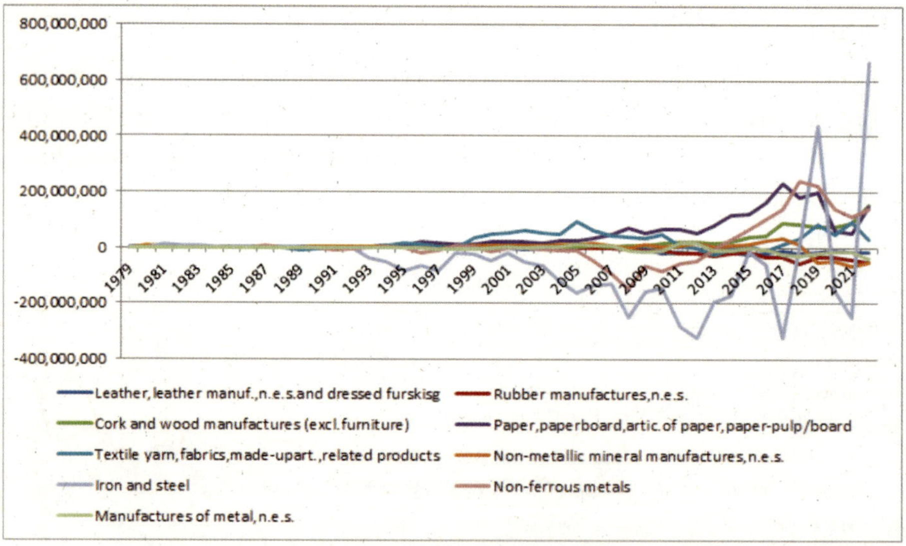

India's surplus in this section ranges from USD 15 million to USD 55 million, with the lowest surplus in manufactured leather products and the highest in manufactured rubber products. Indonesia had positive net export in three other divisions (cork and wood manufactures; paper, paperboard, paper-pulp/board; and non-ferrous metal), ranging from USD 135 million to USD 155 million

Machinery and Transport Equipment

The machinery and transport equipment section has been dominated by India. It had a surplus in six out of nine divisions, with the largest one being in road vehicles (USD 774 million). Indonesia had a surplus in three divisions, ranging from USD 4 million to USD 32 million.

Figure 10

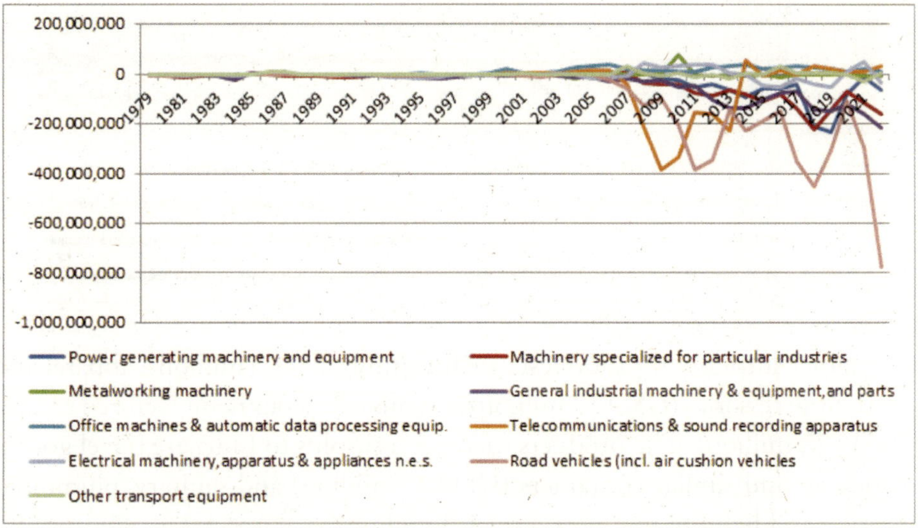

India's exports in electrical machinery, power generating machinery, machinery for particular industries and general industrial machinery showed surpluses at USD 34 million, USD 60 million, USD 158 million and USD 213 million, respectively. Meanwhile, Indonesia had surpluses in office machines and automatic data processing equipment (USD 10 million) and telecommunications and sound recording apparatus products (USD 32 million).

Miscellaneous Manufactured Articles

Among eight divisions of miscellaneous manufactured articles, Indonesia had a surplus in five divisions, while India had a surplus in three. Indonesia's largest surplus was in footwear products (USD 47 million), while India's enjoyed a surplus in photographic apparatus, optical goods and watch products (USD 18.9 million).

Figure 11

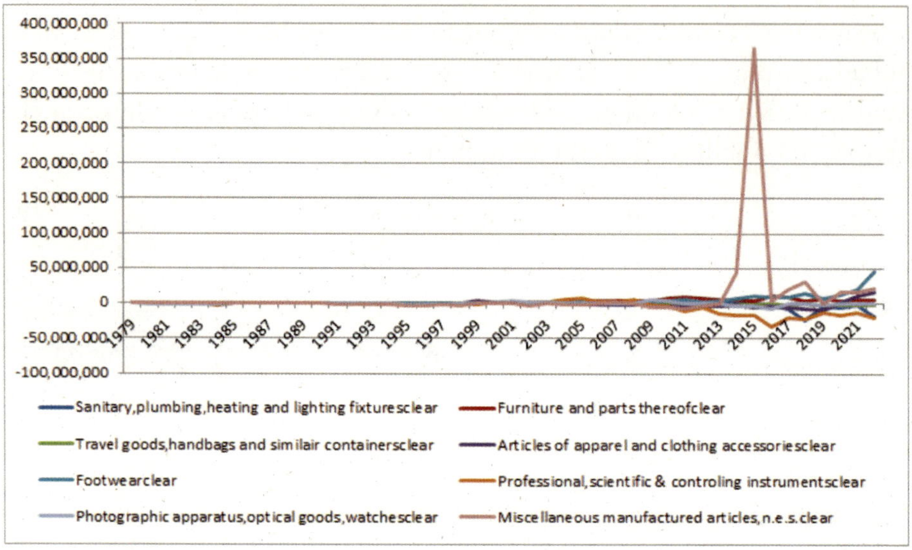

Other surpluses for Indonesia are furniture (USD 5 million), apparel and clothing accessories (USD 17 million) and miscellaneous manufactured articles (USD 22 million). The products that give a surplus to India are travel goods, handbags and similar containers (USD 17 million) and sanitary, plumbing, heating and lighting fixtures (USD 1.8 million).

Conclusion

From the nine divisions of the 2-digit SITC charts above, we can conclude that bilateral trade between Indonesia and India has been very dynamic and balanced. Indonesia's trade surplus mostly came from non-manufactured products such as crude materials, mineral fuels and animal and vegetable oils. On the other hand, India had a surplus mostly from manufactured products such as chemicals and related products, and machinery and transport equipment.

7

India and Indonesia: The Economic Potential

*Sanjay Chadha**

Historical and Economic Context

India and Indonesia, with populations of over 1.4 billion and 273 million respectively, are significant players in the global economy. Their economic partnership is anchored in the shared history of trade and cultural exchanges, dating back to ancient maritime routes. Both countries are members of key regional and international organisations, including the G20, ASEAN-India Summit, and the Indian Ocean Rim Association (IORA).

Being two of Asia's largest economies, India and Indonesia have recognised the potential for economic cooperation and aiming to strengthen their partnership across various sectors. This article explores the key areas of collaboration, including infrastructure development, trade and Investments, IT services, and electric vehicle (EV) technology, while highlighting potential opportunities and future prospects.

Current Scenario and Future Opportunities

A. Infrastructure Development

Current Collaborations

Infrastructure development is a cornerstone of the India-Indonesia economic cooperation. Both countries face similar challenges such as rapid urbanisation, significant population growth and the need for sustainable infrastructure

*Sanjay Chadha is a former Additional Secretary, of Commerce, Govt. of India.

solutions. Collaboration in this sector can drive economic growth, improve connectivity and enhance regional integration.

(i) Transportation and Connectivity

India and Indonesia are investing in projects to improve road, rail and maritime connectivity in Indonesia. They have engaged in various joint infrastructure development projects, reflecting their growing bilateral relations.

One significant project where India has been involved, specifically in providing technical and financial support, is the *Jakarta-Bandung High-Speed Rail Project,* which is aimed at connecting both cities with a high-speed rail network. This network is expected to reduce travel time, boost economic activity and improve connectivity in the region.

Indian automotive companies like Tata Motors, Mahindra & Mahindra, TVS and Royal Enfield have set up units in Indonesia. There is further immense potential for collaboration between both countries, including in the development of ports and airports, which is crucial for boosting trade and tourism, and in the building of smart cities and urban infrastructure which can create opportunities for technology exchange and drive-up investments through joint ventures and partnerships.

(ii) Energy Infrastructure

India is the third largest importer of coal from Indonesia. The 'India-Indonesia Energy Forum' plays an important role in exploring areas of bilateral cooperation in the energy sector. In this context, it is important to note that Indian companies have made substantial investments in Indonesian coal mines.

Both countries are now focussing on renewable energy sources. Investments in energy-efficient infrastructure and technology can reduce dependence on fossil fuels and support sustainable development goals (SDGs). India's expertise in solar energy and Indonesia's potential in geothermal energy offer avenues for collaboration in clean energy projects. Both countries have explored collaborations in renewable energy infrastructure, such as solar and wind energy projects. Indian companies have been involved in setting up solar power plants and wind farms in Indonesia. Prominent Indian companies like Tata Power, Adani Power, L&T, GMR, GVK, Thermax and Essar have already established fully owned subsidiaries/JVs in Indonesia.

Opportunities for Growth

(i) Public-Private Partnerships (PPPs)

Encouraging PPPs can leverage private sector expertise and investment in infrastructure projects. This model can be particularly effective in financing large-scale developments. Collaborative projects can enhance the capacity and efficiency of ports like the Tanjung Priok in Jakarta and the Port of Surabaya, aligning them with international standards.

(ii) Investment in Emerging Cities

With rapid urbanisation, there is significant potential for developing infrastructure in emerging cities, which can drive economic growth and create job opportunities. Collaboration in developing efficient public transportation systems, including metro rail projects and bus rapid transit systems can enhance urban mobility in both countries.

(iii) Technological Innovation

Adopting cutting-edge technologies, such as Artificial Intelligence (AI) and Internet of Things (IoT), can enhance infrastructure efficiency and sustainability. Collaborating on smart Infrastructure solutions can lead to more resilient urban environments.

B. Trade and Investments

Current Collaboration

India and Indonesia began their trade relations in 1978 through the signing of trade agreements, followed by the establishment of a double taxation avoidance agreement in January 1986. The Indo-Indonesia Joint Commission (JCM) was formed in September 2003 and the Double Taxation Avoidance Agreement (DTAA) was endorsed in 2012. Both nations have set an ambitious goal of achieving US$ 50 billion in bilateral trade by 2025.

Some notable initiatives and agreements include:

- The India-Indonesia Comprehensive Economic Partnership Agreement (CEPA) signed in 2011
- The India-ASEAN Free Trade Area (FTA) agreement signed in 2009, which includes Indonesia

- The India-Indonesia Bilateral Investment Treaty (BIT) signed in 2013

(i) Bilateral Trade

India and Indonesia have a significant bilateral trade relationship, with India exporting $4.05 billion to Indonesia and Indonesia exporting $15 billion to India in 2022.

(a) **Main Exported Products:** The main products exported by India to Indonesia primarily include refined petroleum, raw sugar and frozen bovine meat. Indonesia's main exports to India primarily include coal briquettes, palm oil and copper ore.

(b) **Growth Rate:** India's exports to Indonesia have increased at an annualised rate of 42.6 percent between 2017 and 2022, while Indonesia's exports to India have increased at an annualised rate of 94.5 percent in the same period.

(c) **Trade Barriers:** Both countries have agreed to establish a working group to identify and eliminate trade barriers, with India keen on increasing bovine meat exports to Indonesia and wanting higher participation in the pharmaceutical sector.

(ii) Bilateral Investments

(a) **Indonesian investment in India:** India's robust economic growth, its status as the world's most populous nation rank as the fifth-largest global economy, impending approach to a US$ 5 trillion economy, technological advancements, a thriving startup ecosystem and a diversified industrial landscape have piqued Jakarta's keen interest in the Indian market. While Indonesian investment in India remains relatively modest, standing at about US$ 647 million, Indonesian companies have started establishing their presence in various sectors.

(b) **Indian investments in Indonesia:** India's investment in Indonesia stands at US$ 54 billion, primarily channelled through Singapore, with Indian companies like Tata Power, Reliance, Adani and L&T making significant investments in various sectors, including infrastructure, power, textiles, steel, automotive, mining, machinery, banking and consumer goods.

Opportunities for Growth

India and Indonesia have taken several diverse initiatives which will significantly boost bilateral trade and investments.

(i) In 2022, the Reserve Bank of India (RBI) and the Bank Indonesia (BI) signed a Memorandum of Understanding (MoU) to improve mutual cooperation between them.

(ii) A MoU between the National Sugar Institute, Kanpur, and Politeknic Perkebunan LPP, Yogyakarta, was signed during the 7th Joint Commission Meeting (JCM) held in Delhi on June 17, 2022 to enhance cooperation in sugar production.

(iii) The India-Indonesia Economic and Financial Dialogue will look at bilateral investment, financial services and infrastructure development as its areas of cooperation.

(iv) India and Indonesia aim to have real-time settlement and trading in local currencies, as was discussed on the sidelines of the G20 Finance Ministers and Central Bank Governors' meeting last year under India's presidency.

(v) India and Indonesia have jointly declared the commencement of the India-Indonesia Economic and Financial Dialogue (EFD Dialogue) in July 2023. The EFD Dialogue aims to enhance collaboration between both nations, fostering a shared understanding of global issues. It pledges to provide a distinctive platform for mutual learning and policy coordination, thereby reinforcing the commitment to strengthen cooperation.

C. IT Services

Current Collaboration

The IT sector is a vital component of economic cooperation between India and Indonesia. India is a global leader in IT services, while Indonesia is rapidly developing its digital economy. Collaboration in this sector can drive innovation, improve digital literacy and support economic growth.

(i) Digital Transformation

India's expertise in software development and IT services can support Indonesia's digital transformation initiatives, including e-governance, fintech and e-commerce platforms. Indian IT companies like TCS, Tech Mahindra and Newgen Software have set up business units in Indonesia.

Joint efforts in cybersecurity and data protection can also enhance digital infrastructure security.

(ii) Skill Development and Education

Collaborations in IT education and training, through exchange programs and partnerships between educational institutions can foster knowledge sharing and innovation and build a skilled workforce capable of meeting the demands of the global digital economy.

Opportunities for Growth

(i) Start-up Ecosystem

Both countries can benefit from nurturing a vibrant start-up ecosystem, promoting innovation and entrepreneurship in IT, and related fields. Establishing joint incubators and accelerators can support start-ups in both countries, providing them with access to resources, mentorship and funding.

(ii) Cloud Computing and AI

Investment in cloud computing infrastructure and AI technology can drive efficiency and innovation across various sectors, including healthcare, finance and agriculture.

(iii) Digital Payment Systems

India's Unified Payments Interface (UPI) has revolutionised digital payments. Collaboration in this area can help Indonesia enhance its digital payment infrastructure, promoting financial inclusion and reducing transaction costs

D. Electric Vehicle Technology

Current Collaboration

The transition to electric vehicles (EVs) is a significant area of cooperation between India and Indonesia, driven by the need to reduce carbon emissions and promote sustainable transportation. With 115 million two-wheeler vehicles, Indonesia is the largest such market in Southeast Asia as India is in South Asia. Policymakers in Indonesia, like in India, have recognised the importance of these two-wheeler electric vehicles (2W EVs) in the national transportation sector and have prioritised them in the EV transition plans.

The electric two-wheeler industry has the potential to add Indonesian Rupiah 171 trillion in annual economic value and create 215,000 jobs in the component and vehicle manufacturing sector in Indonesia.

To encourage the purchase of these in 2023, Indonesia announced a subsidy of Indonesian rupiah 6.5 million. In Jakarta, policy incentives, such as a subsidy policy of 7 million rupiahs (around $460) on each new electric motorcycle that is locally made, or that has at least 40 percent of its components sourced locally, have been announced.

The focus on electric two wheelers is also logical given the state of infrastructure in the country. Public charging stations in Indonesia are sparse, so home charging with slow chargers, will be the mainstay in the short-term.

Opportunities for Growth

(i) EV Manufacturing

Collaboration in developing affordable EVs can make sustainable transportation accessible to a broader population. Joint ventures in EV manufacturing can leverage India's automotive expertise as also Indonesia's vast natural resources, such as **nickel**, crucial for battery production. Indian automotive companies can establish joint ventures with Indonesian firms to manufacture electric vehicles locally. This can reduce production costs and make EVs more affordable for consumers in both countries.

(ii) Battery Technology

- Both countries can benefit from joint research and development in battery technology, focusing on improving efficiency and reducing costs.
- Investment in battery recycling and waste management can address environmental concerns related to EV production.

(iii) EV Infrastructure Development

Developing EV charging infrastructure is critical for promoting the adoption of electric vehicles. Until 2022, Indonesia had only 439 charging stations and 961 battery swap stations, most of them located in urban areas like Java and Jakarta. The country has set itself a target of installing 31,000 charging stations and 67,000 battery swapping stations by 2030. Public and private sector investment can accelerate this process.

(iv) Policy and Regulatory Framework

- Harmonising policies and regulations can facilitate cross-border investment and innovation in the EV sector.
- Incentives and subsidies can encourage both production and consumption of EVs.

(v) Research and Innovation

Collaborative research initiatives can drive technological advancements, focusing on improving vehicle performance and sustainability. Establishing joint research centres can facilitate collaboration between academic institutions, research organisations and industry players. These centres can focus on developing advanced battery technologies, lightweight materials, and efficient powertrain systems.

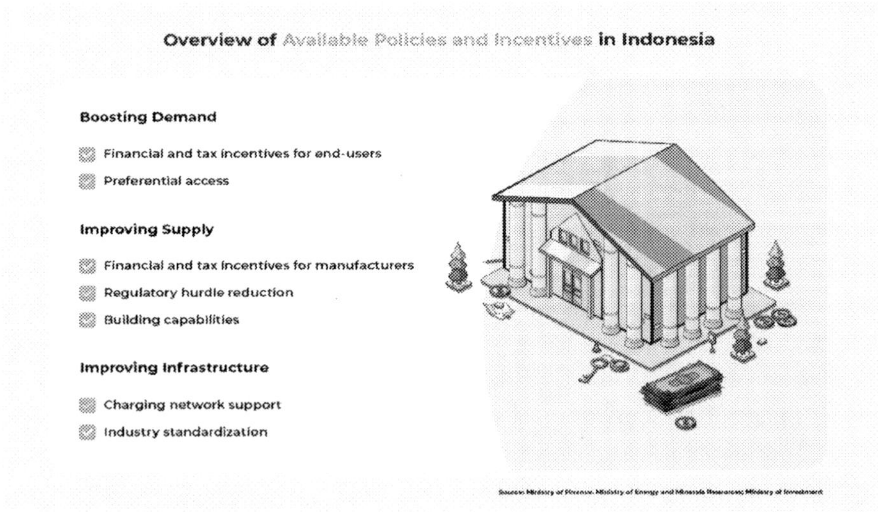

Conclusion

India and Indonesia have a robust foundation for economic cooperation, with significant potential for growth across various sectors. By leveraging their strengths and addressing shared challenges, both can create mutually beneficial opportunities that promote sustainable development and regional stability.

Continued collaboration in infrastructure development, IT services and electric vehicle technology can drive innovation, create jobs, enhance the quality of life for citizens and forge a stronger economic partnership for the future.

To end on a lighter note, on the larger gamut of India-Indonesia cooperation, one may recount an amusing incident that happened at a cultural diplomacy event in Jakarta where Indian and Indonesian diplomats participated in a traditional Balinese dance performance. An Indian diplomat, unfamiliar with the intricate Balinese dance steps, hilariously attempted to follow along, but ended up creating a unique dance style that combined Balinese movements with Bollywood flair. The Indonesian audience enjoyed the fusion so much that they gave it a fun nickname: "Bollywood Bali," celebrating the delightful cross-cultural mix.

8

Defence Diplomacy between Indonesia and India to Maintain Maritime Security in the Indo-Pacific

*Marina Ika Sari**

Introduction

Indonesia and India are maritime neighbours, with the southernmost point of India's Andaman and Nicobar Islands located about 90 nautical miles from Indonesia. Both countries are strategically located maritime powers, with Indonesia as the fulcrum connecting the Indian and Pacific Oceans, and India, occupying a central position in the Indo-Pacific. Indonesia controls vital maritime chokepoints, including the Malacca, Lombok and Sunda Straits, essential for global shipping routes from Asian and African ports to the Far East and the Americas. Similarly, India's unique geographical position straddles all major shipping lanes across the Indian Ocean (Nanda, 2018). In this context, both Indonesia and India can be seen as de facto gatekeepers of a region that handles approximately 60 percent of global maritime trade (Gill, 2023).

Under President Joko Widodo's administration, Indonesia has shifted its national development focus from land-based to maritime orientation. In 2014, President Widodo announced the Global Maritime Fulcrum policy, which is built on five main pillars: (i) Fostering Indonesia's maritime culture; (ii) Protecting the seas and marine resources; (iii) Developing maritime infrastructure and connectivity; (iv) Maritime diplomacy and (v) Building maritime defence capabilities (National Development Planning Agency, 2016).

Considering Indonesia's strategic position with its three Archipelagic Sea

*Marina Ika Sari is a Researcher, The Habibie Center.

Lanes (ALKI) and several choke points, it is crucial to have a robust defence and security system to address maritime threats (Sari, 2017). According to a Defense White Paper (Ministry of Defense of the Republic of Indonesia, 2015, p. 36), one of Indonesia's missions is to transform itself into a self-reliant, advanced and robust maritime nation in alignment with its national interests. As such, President Widodo aims for Indonesia to play a central role in the Indo-Pacific region.

India, which is heavily reliant on maritime routes for international trade, 74 percent of which, is conducted via sea (Singh, 2021), considers its sea lanes as crucial. The most significant maritime transport routes for India are in the Indian Ocean region (Roza, 2015). Given its extensive coastline and dependence on these maritime routes, India prioritises securing them to ensure regional stability. In 2015, Prime Minister Narendra Modi introduced India's maritime vision, Security and Growth for All in the Region (SAGAR), emphasizing safeguarding maritime interests through a secure and stable Indian Ocean Region (Padmaja, 2018). Traditionally, in response to China's growing presence in the Indian Ocean, India has sought to enhance its maritime capabilities and leverage its naval prowess to counterbalance China's influence. Consequently, India's vision includes extending its operational reach from the Indian Ocean to the broader Indo-Pacific to maintain its regional influence.

Indonesia and India established diplomatic relations on March 3, 1951. Bilateral relations progressed notably in 2005 with the signing of a Strategic Partnership agreement, which was later elevated to a Comprehensive Strategic Partnership. In regard to cooperation in the defence sector, Indonesia and India signed a Memorandum of Understanding (MoU) in 1995 (Jha, 2011). The first Agreement on Cooperative Activities in the Field of Defence between the two countries was signed in 2001 and ratified by the Indonesian parliament in December 2006. This agreement was valid until December 2016 (Embassy of India, n.d.).

During Prime Minister Narendra Modi's visit to Jakarta, a new Defence Cooperation Agreement was signed in 2018, replacing the 2001 agreement (Embassy of India, n.d.). Additionally, the Modi-Widodo summit produced the "Shared Vision on Maritime Cooperation in the Indo-Pacific," underscoring both countries' commitment to maritime security and to address defence and security challenges in the Indo-Pacific. This shared vision derives from synergies between India's Act East policy, India's vision of SAGAR and Indonesia's Global Maritime Fulcrum policy (Nanda, 2018).

Indonesia and India face similar security challenges in the region and have expressed concern over China's growing naval presence and assertiveness in the Indo-Pacific (Nanda, 2018). Moreover, both nations must deal with non-traditional security threats in the region, such as human trafficking, arms smuggling, drug trafficking, illegal, unreported and unregulated (IUU) fishing, and terrorism. Consequently, both Indonesia and India are committed to maintaining maritime safety and security for peace, stability and sustainable economic growth in the Indo-Pacific region (Ministry of External Affairs Government of India, 2018).

Maritime security cooperation is a key area of collaboration for Indonesia and India, given their direct borders with the Indian Ocean. Considering their collective interests in safeguarding maritime security, expanding and deepening defence ties is beneficial for Indonesia and India in managing the geopolitical dynamics in the maritime domain effectively. This paper analyses the defence diplomacy activities undertaken by Indonesia and India to leverage opportunities and address challenges collaboratively, aiming to maintain a stable maritime order in the Indo-Pacific.

Conceptual Framework of Defence Diplomacy

Defence diplomacy is a relatively new concept in international relations, emerging prominently in the post-Cold War era as understandings of international security and national security policies evolved. The term "defence diplomacy" was first formally introduced by the United Kingdom (UK) through its 1998 Strategic Defense Review (UK Ministry of Defence). This initiative aimed to integrate military and diplomatic instruments to prevent conflicts, manage crises and address potential disputes with other states (Supriyatno, 2014).

There is no universally accepted definition of defence diplomacy as of now, as the concept is still developing and scholars continue to refine their understanding (Supriyatno, 2014). In general, various experts define defence diplomacy as a method for managing international relations among countries through negotiations specifically focussed on defence issues (Supriyatno, 2014, p. 158).

According to Cottey and Foster (2004, p. 6), defence diplomacy is "the peacetime use of armed forces and related infrastructure (primarily defence ministries) as a tool of foreign and security policy, and more specifically, the use of military cooperation and assistance." Pedrason defines defence diplomacy as all methods and strategies used by countries that, while potentially competitive, engage in practices including economic, cultural, political cooperation, defence cooperation and diplomacy to foster friendships, promote cooperation and, most importantly, build and enhance mutual trust (Pedrason, 2015). The table below depicts various forms of defence diplomacy activities.

Table 1: Defence Diplomacy Activities

• Bilateral and multilateral contacts between senior military and civilian defence officials.
• Appointment of defence attaches to foreign countries.
• Bilateral defence cooperation agreements.
• Training of foreign military and civilian defence personnel.
• Provision of expertise and advice on the democratic control of armed forces, defence management and military technical areas.
• Contacts and exchanges between military personnel and units, and ship visits.
• Placement of military or civilian personnel in partner countries' defence ministries or armed forces.
• Deployment of training teams.
• Provision of military equipment and other material aid.
• Bilateral or multilateral military exercises for training purposes.

Source: Cottey and Foster, 2004.

Defence diplomacy has several key characteristics (Cottey & Forster, 2004; Gindarsah, 2016; Syawfi in Multazam, 2010):

(a) **Strategic Engagement:** Defence diplomacy enables a country to establish strategic relationships with major and middle powers, facilitating broader geopolitical engagement.

(b) **Confidence-Building Measures:** This aspect focuses on fostering good relations between nations, reducing tensions and misunderstandings, and promoting transparency in military capabilities. The goal is to avoid perceptions of threat and build mutual trust between countries.

(c) **Defence Capabilities:** Defence diplomacy aims to enhance a country's security capabilities to address potential threats. This includes cooperation like joint exercises, arms trade, military education and personnel exchanges.

(d) **Defence Industry Development:** This dimension involves collaboration in defence industry projects, technology transfers, licensing and investment in defence sector development.

Defence Diplomacy between Indonesia and India to Strengthen Maritime Security in the Indo-Pacific

Under the Agreement on Cooperative Activities in the Field of Defence, Indonesia and India have been implementing various forms of defence diplomacy at the strategic and operational level.

A. Strategic Level

1. Biennial Defence Minister Forum

The Biennial Defence Ministers' Forum is a high-level meeting between defence ministers of Indonesia and India. It was first held in 2012 (Ministry of Defense, 2014). At the inaugural forum, India's then Defence Minister, A.K. Antony visited Indonesia. He described his meeting with his Indonesian counterpart, Purnomo Yusgiantoro, as a pivotal moment for a promising start. Both countries discussed ways to enhance bilateral defence cooperation. The second forum took place when Indonesian Defence Minister General (Retired) Ryamizard Ryacudu visited India in 2018, where both sides focussed on advancing cooperation in the defence industry and technology (Embassy of India, n.d.). The Biennial Defence Ministers' Forum involves bilateral contact between senior military and civilian defence officials. It provides both Indonesia and India a platform to discuss defence cooperation and address shared security challenges.

2. Joint Defence Cooperation Committee (JDCC)

In 2007, Indonesia and India established a bilateral Joint Defence Cooperation Committee (JDCC) which would be led by defence secretaries of both countries. Between 2007 and 2017, the JDCC met on five occasions (2007, 2010, 2012, 2013 and 2017). During the sixth JDCC in 2018, both sides agreed to initiate bilateral naval exercises and the first such exercise called, 'Samudra Shakti,' took place in November 2018 in Surabaya (Embassy of

India, n.d.). To date, Indonesia and India have conducted seven JDCC meetings, the latest one being in 2024.

The 7th India-Indonesia JDCC meeting was co-chaired by India's Defence Secretary Giridhar Aramane and Indonesia's Secretary General of Defence, Air Marshal Donny Ermawan Taufanto, M.D.S., in New Delhi. During this meeting, both parties expressed satisfaction over the expanding scope of bilateral defence cooperation (Embassy of India, 2023).

The forum's technical aspects are divided into two Joint Working Groups: Joint Working Group I is focussed on defence policy and military cooperation, while Joint Working Group II addresses military facilities, logistics, defence industry and research and development (Ministry of Defense of the Republic of Indonesia, 2012). The co-chairs also review progress on various bilateral defence cooperation initiatives discussed in these working groups. Additionally, Indonesia and India have agreed to enhance collaboration in the defence industry, maritime security and multilateral cooperation (Embassy of India, 2023).

3. Navy-to-Navy Talks (NTNT)

Navy-to-Navy Talks (NTNT) is a forum held biennially to discuss military cooperation between the Indonesian and Indian Navies. Collaboration in NTNT includes maritime security, coordinated patrols, hydrographic cooperation, education and exchange programmes, joint exercises, ship visits and information sharing (Sari, 2017). To date, Indonesia and India have conducted 11 NTNT meetings, the most recent of which was held in New Delhi.

According to defence diplomacy concepts outlined by Cottey and Foster, the NTNT represents a form of defence diplomacy characterised by contacts and exchanges between military personnel and units, as well as ship visits, specifically between the two navies. The NTNT is seen as one of the most advanced and significant forms of defence diplomacy and highlights the close relationship between both navies. Through direct interactions and dialogues, Indonesia and India can enhance confidence-building measures (CBMs) and strengthen military cooperation to maintain maritime security stability.

4. India-Indonesia Security Dialogue (IISD)

During President Joko Widodo's state visit to India on December 12-13, 2016, leaders of Indonesia and India agreed to establish the India-Indonesia Security Dialogue (IISD) to develop a comprehensive action plan for security cooperation (Embassy of India, n.d.). The IISD is a forum that brings together the Coordinating Minister for Political, Legal and Security Affairs of Indonesia and the National Security Advisor of India to discuss and enhance cooperation on political and security issues (Ministry of External Affairs, Government of India, 2022).

The inaugural IISD meeting was held in India in 2018. The second IISD meeting took place in Indonesia in 2022, with the aim of strengthening Comprehensive Strategic Partnership in areas of security and connectivity. During this meeting, Indonesia and India discussed global and security issues, including counter-terrorism and violent extremism, and explored opportunities to enhance cooperation in maritime security, defence, space and cyber security (Tempo, 2022).

B. Operational Level

1. India-Indonesia Coordinated Patrol (Ind-Indo Corpat)

The India-Indonesia Coordinated Patrol (Ind-Indo Corpat) is a coordinated maritime patrol conducted by the Indonesian and Indian Navies. It was initiated in 2002 to ensure maritime security and safety on the borders of both countries. This patrol is conducted twice a year and, as of May 2024, has reached its 42nd edition. Ind-Indo Corpat takes place in the Andaman Sea, which borders Indonesia and India. The Andaman Sea is strategically significant due to its proximity to the northern entrance of the Malacca Strait, a key chokepoint for international shipping and trade (Mukherjee, 2016).

Coordinated patrols differ from joint patrols operationally. Coordinated patrols are conducted along the border areas of each country, with both nations coordinating and reporting conditions during the operation. In contrast, joint patrols involve entering a specific location and conducting patrols together. The Ind-Indo Corpat involves operations within the jurisdictional waters of each country, focussing on preventive measures such as early threat detection and inspections of maritime users (Sari, 2017).

The 42nd edition of Ind-Indo Corpat was conducted in Sabang, Indonesia, in May 2024, marking a significant milestone in India-Indonesia maritime partnership. The operation aims to address various maritime violations, including smuggling, piracy, hijacking, illegal fishing and drug and human trafficking. Through a combination of official engagements, cultural interactions and strategic planning, both nations reaffirmed their commitment to ensuring the security and stability of the Indian Ocean Region (Sharma, 2024).

The Ind-Indo Corpat represents one of the most advanced and significant forms of defence diplomacy for both countries. It aims to enhance coordination and interoperability while strengthening the relationship between the Indonesian and Indian Navies. The success of this long-standing coordinated patrol underscores the importance of bilateral initiatives in fostering international maritime cooperation and security for all. (Sharma, 2024).

2. Samudra Shakti Exercise

Established in 2018, the Samudra Shakti Exercise is a bilateral naval exercise conducted between Indonesia and India. The exercise comprises two phases: the Harbour Phase and the Sea Phase. The Harbour Phase includes cross-deck visits, professional interactions, subject matter expert exchanges and sports activities. The Sea Phase features weapon firing, helicopter operations, anti-submarine warfare, air defence exercises, and boarding operations. The inaugural exercise took place in November 2018 in Surabaya, Indonesia. Subsequent editions were held in Visakhapatnam and the Bay of Bengal in November 2019, Jakarta, Indonesia, the Sunda Straits in September 2021 and in Batam, Indonesia in May 2023 (Embassy of India, n.d.).

The Samudra Shakti Exercise aims to enhance mutual understanding, jointness, cooperation and interoperability in maritime security operations between the Indonesian and Indian Navies. Additionally, it serves as a platform for exchanging best practices and developing a shared understanding (Lantamal IV, 2023). Ultimately, these exercises can strengthen bilateral ties between both countries and underscore their shared commitment to peace and stability in the Indo-Pacific region (Ministry of Defense of India, 2023).

Samudra Shakti is a form of defence diplomacy between Indonesia and

India, characterised by bilateral military exercises for training purposes. This joint exercise represents the newest form of military cooperation at the operational level. Enhanced collaboration in such exercises can increase the defence capabilities of both nations, particularly in developing the skills and professionalism of their military personnel.

Conclusion

Under the Agreement on Cooperative Activities in the Field of Defence framework, defence diplomacy between Indonesia and India to maintain maritime security in the Indo-Pacific can be classified into strategic and operational levels. At the strategic level, both countries engage in several bilateral security dialogues at various tiers. These include Biennial Meetings at the level of the Ministers of Defence, the JDCC at the level of the Secretary-General, the IISD at the level of the Coordinating Minister for Politics and Security, and NTNT at the level of naval officers. At the operational level, Indonesia and India conduct programs such as the Ind-Indo Corpat and the Samudra Shakti Exercise.

As mentioned above, the defence diplomacy activities conducted by Indonesia and India contribute to strategic engagement, build CBMs, and enhance the defence capabilities for both nations. Various forums facilitate interaction, communication and coordination among officials from defence ministries and military officers, fostering mutual trust. Additionally, coordinated patrols and joint military exercises can develop and improve the defence capabilities of both countries, specifically developing skills and professionalism of the Indonesian and Indian navies in field operations.

Over time, Indonesia-India defence diplomacy has evolved significantly, with notable advancements related to bilateral naval activities. In addition to bolstering existing cooperation, both nations have established new platforms, such as the IISD and the Samudra Shakti Exercise. Ultimately, implementing defence diplomacy will enhance Indonesia-India bilateral ties and underscore their shared commitment to maintain peace and stability in the Indo-Pacific region. With robust defence cooperation in place, it is hoped that Indonesia and India will continue to explore opportunities for collaboration to advance their mutual maritime security interests.

REFERENCES

Cottey, A., & Foster, A. (2004). *Reshaping Defence Diplomacy: New Roles for Military Cooperation and Assistance.* Oxford University Press.

Embassy of India. (2023, May 3). *Defence Secretary & Secretary General of MoD, Indonesia Agree to Enhance Collaboration in Areas of Defence Industry, Maritime Security & Multilateral Cooperation.* Embassy of India. https://www.indianembassyjakarta.gov.in/press? id=eyJpdiI6IkUyaXdWUk VFZUtGZTcxcj ZBQWl6SWc9PSIsInZhbHVlIjoiVUlSanZVS1pON lVmdzNDK1h0 UmtCQT09IiwibWFj IjoiNDQyMmY wMGMzNzliMDkyMWFjZDY2ZDkwMzN kNzAyZThkN2ZkNjdjMmY5ZGYwNGQwYWNjOGFhMmYxZmI3M2Y3YyJ9

Embassy of India. (n.d.). *India-Indonesia Bilateral Brief.* Embassy of India. https://www.indian embassyjakarta.gov.in/pages?id=eyJpdiI6IllhbDhiNHpFa0JrdHVEdVcrb 0l5dkE9P SIs In ZhbHVlIjoiakh3RG9WT1kyTjhhWXNLUlZkS1VxQ T09IiwibWFjIjoiNzdmOTZl ZWU 4ZGIxNWRkZjBiYTk5MWE0NmUyZmI3YzA4YzEyYmY2YmU5MT QwZTkzNzVk YW E3 MDRhMDI3OTBhZiJ9&subid=eyJpdiI6IjhvRGlzXC9Ma HhIbFBST HlUeH RrTV JR PT0iLCJ2YWx1ZSI6I jQ2XC81U29cL29jNFwvUXdPcUhmR2xkc2c9PSIsIm1hYyI6 Im Fk ZTMy MTc2ZTdmNmYzOTBlYThk ODdjMWE4NWN mO TV lN zdlM GRi M2 M0 NDBlM zE5Njg3MGQxMzdkODI0ZWM 4NDgifQ==&nextid=eyJpdiI6IkxCaDI3dmNq M3VSM1FrdWtqbEJLRkE9 PSIsInZhbHVlIjoi WnZQQ1wvUjc0R3d0 UEdyTUE3XC9N STVRPT0iLCJtYWMiOiI0MzI0MmJkMmFlNmE0NT I0MjY0MjYwNzdjZDFkZTg5Nm MxOTc3NzIzZjY2MTYzNGUxYWI1ZGU2MWRlOTlkYThkIn0=

Gill, D.M. (2023, March 2). *Bolstering Indonesia-India Strategic Partnership Will Be Mutually Beneficial.* The Jakarta Post. https://www.thejakartapost.com/opinion/2023/03/02/bolstering-indonesia-india-strategic-partnership-will-be-mutually-beneficial.html

Gindarsah, I. (2016). Strategic Hedging in Indonesia's Defense Diplomacy. *Defense & Security Analysis,* 32(4), 336-354. Taylor & Francis Journals.

Jha, P. K. (2011). India's Defence Diplomacy in Southeast Asia. *Journal of Defence Studies,* 5(1), 47-63. Institute for Defence Studies and Analyses.

Lantamal IV. (2023, May 14). *Pererat Kerjasama Bilateral, Kapal Perang India INS Kavaratti-P31 dan KRI Sultan Iskandar Muda-367 Mulai Latihan di Batam.* Lantamal IV. https://lantamal4-koarmada1.tnial.mil.id/berita/7024/PERERAT-KERJASAMA-BILATERAL,-KAPAL-PERANG-INDIA-INS-KAVARATTI-P31-DAN-KRI-SULTAN-ISKANDAR-MUDA-367-MULAI-LATIHAN-DI-BATAM/

Ministry of Defense of India. (2023, May 14). *India-Indonesia Bilateral Exercise Samudra Shakti-23.* Ministry of Defense of India. https://pib.gov.in/PressReleaseIframePage.aspx?PRID =1924058

Ministry of Defense of the Republic of Indonesia. (2012). *Sekjen Kemhan Pimpin The 3rd Indonesia India Joint Defence Cooperation Committee Meeting.* Ministry of Defense of the Republic of Indonesia. http://dmc.dephan.go.id/postsekjen-kemhan-pimpin-the-3rd-indonesia-india-joint-defencecooperation-committee-meeting.html

Ministry of Defense of the Republic of Indonesia. (2015). *Buku Putih Pertahanan Indonesia.* Ministry of Defense of the Republic of Indonesia. https://www.kemhan.go.id/wp-content/uploads/2022/08/BUKU-PUTIH.pdf

Ministry of External Affairs Government of India. (2018, May 30). *Shared Vision of India-Indonesia Maritime Cooperation in the Indo-Pacific.* Ministry of External Affairs Government of India.

https://www.mea.gov.in/bilateral-documents.htm?dtl/29933/Shared_Vision_of_India Indonesia_Maritime_Cooperation_in_the_IndoPacific

Ministry of External Affairs, Government of India. (2022, March 17). *Second India-Indonesia Security Dialogue.* Ministry of External Affairs, Government of India. https://www.mea.gov.in/press-releases.htm?dtl/34982/Second_India_Indonesia_Security_Dialogue

Mukherjee, A. (2016). The Unsinkable Aircraft Carrier: The Andaman and Nicobar Command. In A. Mukherjee, & C. R. Rohan, *India's Naval Strategy and Asian Security* (pp. 86-105). Routledge.

Multazam, A. (2010). *Diplomasi Pertahanan Indonesia Terhadap Korea Selatan Periode 2006-2009.* Universitas Indonesia.

Nanda, B. (2018). India and Indonesia Affirm a Shared Vision of Maritime Cooperation in the Indo-Pacific. *DPG Policy Brief,* 3(8), 1-4. Delhi Policy Group. https://www.delhipolicygroup.org/uploads_dpg/publication_file/india-and-indonesia-affirm-a-shared-vision-of-maritime-cooperation-in-the-indo-pacific-1100.pdf

National Development Planning Agency. (2016, March 8). *Mewujudkan Indonesia Sebagai Poros Maritim Dunia.* National Development Planning Agency. https://www.bappenas.go.id/id/berita/mewujudkan-indonesia-sebagai-poros-maritim-dunia

Padmaja, G. (2018, April 25). *Revisiting "SAGAR" – India's Template for Cooperation in the Indian Ocean Region.* National Maritime Foundation. https://maritimeindia.org/revisiting-sagar-indias-template-for-cooperation-in-the-indian-ocean-region/#_ftn3

Pedrason, R. (2015). *ASEAN's Defence Diplomacy: The Road to Southeast Asian Defence Community.* Heidelberg University.

Roza, R. (2015). Doktrin Poros Maritim Dunia dan Hubungan Indonesia-India. In P. P. Nainggolan, *Agenda Poros Maritim Dunia dan Perubahan Lingkungan Strategis* (pp. 81-82). P3DI Setjen DPR RI & Azza Grafika.

Sari, M. I. (2017). *Diplomasi Pertahanan Indonesia terhadap India atas Kepentingan Nasional Indonesia di Samudera Hindia.* Universitas Pertahanan Indonesia.

Sharma, N. (2024). *Ind-Indo Corpat Exercise 2024, Elements of Ind-Indo Corpat.* PW Centres. https://www.pw.live/exams/defence/ind-indo-corpat-exercise-2024/

Singh, A. J. (2021, February 27). *India's Maritime Economy: Driving India's Growth.* India Foundation. https://indiafoundation.in/articles-and-commentaries/indias-maritime-economy-driving-indias-growth/#:~:text=About%2095%25%20of%20India's%20trade,two%20 strategically % 20located%20island%20territories

Supriyatno, M. (2014). *Tentang Ilmu Pertahanan.* Yayasan Obor.

Tempo (2022, March 18). *India dan Indonesia Dialog Soal Keamanan.* Tempo. https://dunia.tempo.co/read/1572276/india-dan-indonesia-dialog-soal-keamanan

9

Factoring ASEAN and IORA in Strengthening India-Indonesia Relations

*Dr. Rahul Mishra**

Introduction

India and Indonesia are considered two of the most significant countries in the Indo-Pacific region and the wider Global South, not just due to their geographical size but also because of their strong economic and strategic potential. The two countries have witnessed remarkable growth over the last few decades. The bilateral relationship between these two rising powers, which are also two of the largest democracies, is essential in maintaining peace and stability in the Indo-Pacific region. In recent years, regional multilateral organisations such as the Association of Southeast Asian Nations (ASEAN) and Indian Ocean Rim Association (IORA), have played a crucial role in strengthening relations between India and Indonesia. Today, both India and Indonesia have emerged as the leading powers of the Global South, which is also manifested in their pivotal roles in the G-20.[1]

This article examines how regional organisations, ASEAN and IORA, have facilitated stronger relations between the two countries. It examines their strategic importance, contributions to Delhi-Jakarta bonhomie, the obstacles they face, and their potential, moving forward.

*Dr Rahul Mishra is an Associate Professor at Jawaharlal Nehru University, New Delhi.

India-Indonesia Relations: A Historical Context

India and Indonesia have a rich historical past dating back to more than a millennia. The ancient linkages between these two 'Mosaics of Cultures'[2] was established through trade and commerce, cultural exchanges, and the promotion of shared religious beliefs, Hinduism and Buddhism, and later Islam, facilitated by the Indian Ocean that acted as a bridge between India and its Southeast Asian neighbour.[3] These linkages are evident in the shared cultural heritage and practices in Indonesia – most notably in the form of the famous Borobudur Temple in Indonesia and the Bali Jatra in India's Odisha.[4]

During Indonesia's struggle for independence, Nehru organised the *Southeast Asia Day* in Lucknow on October 24, 1945. Later, in 1947, Nehru organised the *Asian Relations Conference*, and the *Conference on Indonesia* in 1949, in which Indonesia was at the centre-stage. Soon after their independence, India and Indonesia established diplomatic ties. The Bandung Conference 1955, served as an important milestone towards Afro-Asian solidarity.[5] The leaders of both countries – Jawaharlal Nehru of India and Sukarno of Indonesia – played instrumental roles in the formation of the Non-Aligned Movement (NAM). This enabled them in fostering closer ties.

However, differences between Nehru and Sukarno, and subsequent policy divergences during and after Indonesia's Konfrontasi exacerbated the systemic constraints imposed by the Cold War, drifting the two countries away from each other. The end of the Cold War led to a period of increased emphasis on economic liberalisation and regional connectivity, which helped reinvigorate India's relationship with Indonesia. With the emergence of the Indo-Pacific construct, the role of regional institutions, such as G-20, ASEAN and IORA, in fostering stronger ties between India and Indonesia have become more pronounced.[6]

The cooperation between India and Indonesia spans over wide range of issues, including trade and commerce, people to people linkages, cultural and educational ties, efforts in boosting infrastructure and connectivity, maintaining regional peace, and strategic cooperation. Their engagement through ASEAN framework takes this long-standing relation into a multilateral framework their concerns and interests converge. Moreover, the geographical proximity between the two countries makes them critically important for each other on strategic, military, connectivity, and economic fronts alike. It may be noted that the distance between Andaman & Nicobar islands and Indonesia's Aceh is only about 80 nautical miles.

Indonesia, the largest archipelagic state in the world, and India, with its extensive coastline straddling the Bay of Bengal and the Indian Ocean, view the oceanic region as integral to their national security and economic interests. Their participation in IORA reflects a commitment to promote cooperative strategies for ensuring regional peace, prosperity, and sustainable development.[7] As IORA members, India and Indonesia recognise the Indian Ocean's strategic importance, which serves as a vital conduit for global trade and energy supplies.

ASEAN: A Catalyst for India-Indonesia Cooperation

In 1992, India launched the "Look East Policy" which laid down the foundation of its relationship with ASEAN.[8] The Look East Policy later evolved into the "Act East Policy" in 2014 under Prime Minister Narendra Modi's government.[9] This policy underscores ASEAN's strategic importance as India's gateway for broader engagement with Southeast Asia and in the broader Indo-Pacific region. Notably, ASEAN is a crucial partner for India in efforts to foster regional integration, promote trade, and enhance maritime cooperation. India's engagement with ASEAN is a cornerstone of India's Look East and subsequent Act East Policies.[10] Since 1993, ASEAN has provided India with a platform to enhance ties with its member states.

Considered primus inter pares in Southeast Asia, and as one of ASEAN's founding members, Indonesia yields considerable influence in ASEAN, which has been manifested through its leading role in promoting regional stability, security, and economic integration.[11] This was particularly evident during ASEAN's 2012 diplomatic crisis in Cambodia and Marty Natalegawa's shuttle diplomacy, and the 2021 Myanmar crisis when the Indonesian foreign minister played a key role in setting up a troika to deal with the Myanmar issue.[12] Thus, Indonesia's leadership in ASEAN has enabled it to foster closer relations with India, particularly through frameworks, like the ASEAN-India Summit and the East Asia Summit (EAS). Despite India opting out of RCEP, the economic dialogue within ASEAN continues to provide opportunities for trade and investment cooperation between India and ASEAN member countries including Indonesia.[13]

Additionally, ASEAN-led institutions such as the ASEAN Defence Ministers' Meeting (ADMM) Plus and the ASEAN Regional Forum (ARF) have provided greater avenues for multilateral and bilateral consultations. Given the escalating threats of terrorism, piracy, and maritime security, both countries have demonstrated a strong commitment to preserving peace and security in the Indo-Pacific.

Furthermore, Indonesia's pivotal location at the Malacca Straits – one of the busiest maritime commerce routes in the world – satisfies India's interests in preserving freedom of navigation and advancing a rules-based maritime order. India and Indonesia are working closely on enhancing maritime domain awareness, capacity-building, and naval exercises through ASEAN-led efforts, resulting in increased security in the Indo-Pacific region.

Indian Ocean Rim Association (IORA): A Key Forum for Maritime Cooperation

Established in 1997, the IORA is an inter-governmental organisation that promotes cooperation among littoral countries of the Indian Ocean.[14] It focuses on a wide range of issues, including maritime security, trade and investment, Humanitarian Assistance and Disaster Relief (HADR) efforts, scientific and technological cooperation, and the sustainable development of marine resources. Both India and Indonesia have been active IORA members, and have intensified their engagement with the organisation in recent years.

Widely recognised as a leading example of 'open regionalism' IORA serves as a key forum for regional cooperation, particularly in the context of emerging challenges such as piracy, transnational crime, and growing geopolitical tensions in these waters. India and Indonesia share concerns over issues such as maritime piracy in the Indian Ocean, gun running, human trafficking, illegal fishing, and increasing militarisation of the region by external powers. As such, their partnership within the IORA is focused on addressing these security threats while promoting regional stability and economic growth.

India and Indonesia's Role in IORA

India has consistently highlighted the significance of the IORA in promoting trade, security, and connectivity in the region. It has worked to enhance maritime cooperation with member states, especially Indonesia, in line with its Sagar Mala initiative and Indo-Pacific Oceans Initiative (IPOI).[15,16]

So far as Indonesia is concerned, keeping with Indonesian President Joko Widodo's goal of developing Indonesia as the world's biggest archipelago, Indonesia uses IORA as a platform to promote its maritime identity. The IORA has enabled India and Indonesia to expand their economic and maritime cooperation beyond bilateral ties. Both countries recognise the Indian Ocean's strategic importance for regional trade and commerce, energy security, and as a zone of peace. Through IORA's initiatives, India and Indonesia have enhanced maritime infrastructure, connectivity, and sustainable fisheries management while also combatting a range of non-traditional security threats.

The IORA provides a platform for India and Indonesia to address emerging maritime challenges, such as illegal, unreported, and unregulated (IUU) fishing, human trafficking, and marine pollution.[17] Collaborative efforts on maritime security are vital to ensure that the Indian Ocean remains a region of peace, stability, and prosperity.

The IORA's focus on disaster risk management and climate change adaptation has allowed both countries to cooperate on it. As two countries that are highly vulnerable to natural disasters such as Tsunami and cyclones, they have sought to enhance their respective disaster preparedness and response capabilities through IORA-linked HADR mechanisms. For instance, the 2004 Indian Ocean tsunami and 2008 cyclone Nargis in Myanmar highlighted the need for greater regional cooperation in disaster preparedness and relief efforts.

Furthermore, the IORA has promoted the sharing of best practices and technical expertise between India, Indonesia, and other member states, leading to improved coordination in the occurrence of natural disasters.[18] Climate change mitigation is also a shared priority for both India and Indonesia. Their participation in IORA's initiatives to protect marine biodiversity and promote renewable energy sources showcase their commitment in this regard.

Being maritime nations with vast coastlines, India and Indonesia have a vested interest in ensuring the freedom of navigation, security of sea lanes, and sustainable development of ocean resources. Both countries have championed initiatives aimed at strengthening regional cooperation in these areas within the IORA.

Maritime security is a cornerstone of India-Indonesia cooperation within the IORA framework. As mentioned above, the Indian Ocean is a critical transit point for global trade and energy supplies, making it vulnerable to threats such as piracy, terrorism, and smuggling. Consequently, both countries have taken proactive measures to address these challenges through bilateral and multilateral initiatives.

The rise of piracy in the Indian Ocean, particularly off the coast of Somalia, has been a major concern for both India and Indonesia. Keeping this in view, both countries are working together to combat piracy through coordinated patrols, intelligence sharing, and capacity-building programs for smaller island states in the region. Notably, the Indian and the Indonesian Navies have conducted joint exercises and maritime patrols to enhance their ability to respond to regional security threats.[19] This collaboration reflects a shared commitment to ensure the safety of sea lanes and maintaining a rules-based order in the Indian Ocean and the wider Indo-Pacific region.

India and Indonesia have a shared commitment to upholding the principle of freedom of navigation in the Indian Ocean, in accordance with the international laws and conventions. This has become particularly important in the light of increasing presence of external powers in the region, such as China, whose naval activities have raised concerns about potential conflicts and challenges to the existing maritime order. Both India and Indonesia have emphasised the need for a rules-based maritime order that respects the sovereignty of coastal states and promotes peaceful dispute resolution.

Further, India and Indonesia have also played key roles in promoting regional security cooperation through the IORA's Maritime Safety and Security Working Group.[20] This platform facilitates the sharing of best practices, capacity building, and the development of regional frameworks to address maritime security challenges. Both countries' initiatives have helped in creating a more secure and stable maritime environment in the Indian Ocean.

Economic cooperation is another vital component of India-Indonesia relations within the IORA framework. As two large economies in the region, India and Indonesia have played a leadership role in advocating for greater economic cooperation through IORA's Economic Cooperation Working Group.[21] The group focuses on identifying opportunities for trade and investment, improving regional infrastructure, and facilitating the movement of goods and services across borders.

Both countries recognise the importance of enhancing regional economic integration and promoting sustainable development in the Indian Ocean region. Thus, they have been working to boost trade and investment among IORA member states by reducing barriers to market access and promoting regional economic integration.

India and Indonesia are committed to promoting the sustainable use of Indian Ocean marine resources. Over and illegal fishing, marine pollution and adverse effects of climate change constitute significant threats to the long-term viability of the ocean's ecosystem. Through the IORA's Blue Economy initiatives, India and Indonesia have worked together to promote sustainable fishing practices, protect marine biodiversity, and support the development of eco-friendly technologies for ocean-based industries.

Additionally, Indonesia, with its vast archipelago and rich marine resources, has been a strong advocate for the Blue Economy.[22] India, too, has supported these efforts by providing technical assistance and expertise in marine science and technology. Both countries recognise the importance of balancing economic growth with environmental sustainability, and have promoted regional cooperation in this sphere through IORA's Fisheries Support Unit and Working Group on the Blue Economy.

Environmental protection and disaster risk management are also key areas of India-Indonesia cooperation within the IORA.[23] As mentioned above, both countries are highly vulnerable to natural disasters such as tsunamis, cyclones and rising sea levels due to climate change. Their cooperation in this domain reflects a shared commitment to enhance regional resilience and mitigate the impacts of natural disasters.

Further, climate change poses a significant threat to the Indian Ocean region, with rising sea levels, increasing temperatures, and more frequent extreme weather events. To address that, IORA members, including India and Indonesia, have worked together by promoting climate adaptation strategies, supporting regional efforts to reduce greenhouse gas emissions, and advocating for greater international climate action cooperation. Both countries have also collaborated on initiatives aimed at protecting the marine environment from pollution, particularly plastic and industrial waste. India and Indonesia have expressed a strong commitment to reduce marine pollution and have supported regional efforts to improve waste management and promote sustainable practices in ocean-based industries.

Given their vulnerability to natural disasters, India and Indonesia have also prioritised disaster risk management within the IORA framework. Both countries have supported the development of regional early warning systems, disaster response mechanisms, and capacity-building programs to enhance the resilience of the member states. India's National Disaster Management Authority (NDMA) and Indonesia's National Agency for Disaster Management (BNPB) have played key roles in providing technical assistance and training to other IORA countries.

As leading powers in the Indian Ocean region, India and Indonesia have advocated for a stronger multilateral approach to regional governance. That includes strong efforts to promote the IORA as a key platform for dialogue and cooperation on regional issues, emphasising the importance of inclusivity and consensus-based decision-making. Both countries have also sought to enhance the IORA's role in addressing non-traditional security threats, such as human trafficking, drug smuggling, and maritime terrorism. Both are promoting multilateral cooperation on these issues.

Trilateral Dialogue on Indian Ocean (TDIO): A Strategic Framework for Regional Cooperation

The Indian Ocean, considered the world's third-largest ocean (27,243,000 square miles or 70.56 million square km), is a critical maritime domain that serves as a lifeline for global trade and commerce, energy supplies, and tourism. It connects the Middle East, Africa, and South Asia with Southeast Asia and beyond, facilitating the movement of around 80 percent of the world's seaborne oil. Over the past few decades, the Indian Ocean region has emerged as an important stage for great power competition, regional cooperation, and strategic dialogue. In this context, the Trilateral Dialogue on the Indian Ocean (TDIO) forms a vital platform that fosters collaboration among key stakeholders in the region.[24]

The TDIO, established as a dialogue mechanism, brings together India, Australia, and Indonesia – three countries with shared interests in the security, stability, and prosperity of the Indian Ocean region. The trilateral arrangement aims to promote peace, security, and economic growth by addressing shared concerns, enhancing maritime security, and fostering regional cooperation.

Origins and Strategic Rationale

The establishment of the TDIO can be traced back to the growing realisation by India, Australia, and Indonesia of the need for a more focussed, sector-specific minilateral cooperation in the Indian Ocean. Each of these countries plays a critical role in maintaining the security of oceanic region, with India being the dominant maritime power in the Northern Indian Ocean, Australia in the eastern part of the ocean, and Indonesia strategically located at the crossroads between the Indian and Pacific Oceans. A key purpose of establishing TDIO was to give a greater sense of direction to IORA as well since these three countries formed the troika of IORA chairmanship in recent years.

Historically, the Indian Ocean region has been marked by informal bilateral dialogues and collaborations. However, the evolving nature of geopolitical dynamics, particularly the rise of China and its increasing influence in the Indian Ocean, necessitated a range of minilateral and multilateral approaches to counterbalance external influences. The TDIO, therefore, represents a natural progression from bilateral engagements to a trilateral format that seeks to enhance synergies between India, Australia, and Indonesia. The dialogue was formalised in 2017, with the first meeting held in New Delhi.[25] Since then, it has evolved as an important platform for strategic discussions on maritime security, regional connectivity, and economic collaboration.

Objectives of TDIO

The primary objectives of the TDIO are multifaceted, aiming to address the strategic, security, and economic concerns of the region. These objectives include, but not confined to maritime security cooperation, bolstering trade and economic linkages, climate change and sustainable development, promoting a rules-based maritime order, accelerating Humanitarian Assistance and Disaster Relief (HADR) efforts, fostering cooperation in blue economy and sustainable development sectors, strengthening regional connectivity, enhancing Maritime Domain Awareness (MDA), and in collectively tackling terrorism and counterpiracy.

The Indian Ocean region is prone to a range of maritime security threats, including piracy, illegal fishing, drug trafficking, and human smuggling. The

TDIO aims to enhance maritime domain awareness, improve the capabilities of maritime forces, and ensure freedom of navigation in line with international law, particularly the United Nations Convention on the Law of the Sea (UNCLOS).[26]

India, Australia, and Indonesia are committed to upholding a rules-based international order in the Indian Ocean. Through the TDIO, the three countries work together to ensure that international laws governing the high seas are respected, particularly in the context of territorial disputes and freedom of navigation.[27] This has become particularly important in light of the growing influence of China's Belt and Road Initiative (BRI) and the militarisation of critical maritime chokepoints.

To facilitate trade, investment, and infrastructure development, TDIO has emphasised enhancing regional connectivity. India, Australia, and Indonesia have recognised the importance of improving port infrastructure, maritime transportation networks, and digital connectivity to bolster regional economic growth.

The TDIO serves as a platform for deepening economic cooperation in the Indian Ocean region. India, Australia, and Indonesia are key players in global trade, and their cooperation can lead to enhanced economic integration, especially in sectors such as maritime transport, energy security, and blue economy initiatives.

Given the environmental vulnerabilities to the Indian Ocean, especially with the impact of climate change on small island states, the TDIO places a strong emphasis on sustainable development. The dialogue provides a forum for three countries to collaborate on disaster risk management, climate change mitigation, and the promotion of sustainable fisheries and marine ecosystems.

One of the critical areas of collaboration under the TDIO is enhancing maritime domain awareness, which refers to the effective monitoring and management of maritime activities in the region.[28] India, Australia, and Indonesia are working together to share information, conduct joint patrols, and enhance interoperability of their maritime forces to counter maritime threats, including piracy and illegal fishing. The Indian Navy's Information Fusion Centre for the Indian Ocean Region (IFC-IOR) plays a pivotal role in facilitating the sharing of real-time maritime information.[29]

The Indian Ocean region is prone to natural disasters such as tsunamis, cyclones, and earthquakes. Therefore, the TDIO emphasizes cooperation in humanitarian assistance and disaster relief (HADR) operations. India, Australia, and Indonesia are well-positioned to provide timely assistance in the event of natural disasters, facilitate joint exercises and capacity-building initiatives to improve response mechanisms.

The threat of terrorism and piracy in the Indian Ocean region is a major concern for coastal states. The TDIO provides a platform for the three countries to coordinate efforts to combat these threats. Joint naval exercises, intelligence sharing, and capacity-building programs constitutes key components of their cooperation in this area.

The TDIO also focuses on promoting the blue economy, which refers to the sustainable use of ocean resources for economic growth, improved livelihoods, and environmental sustainability. India, Australia, and Indonesia are committed to supporting sustainable fishing practices, protecting marine biodiversity, and investing in ocean-based renewable energy projects such as offshore wind farms and tidal energy.

Conclusion

India and Indonesia's cooperation in the strategic domain, both bilaterally and within ASEAN frameworks, is vital for regional stability. Both countries have a shared interest in maintaining peace and security in the Indo-Pacific. The Indian Ocean, which connects the two countries, is critical for global trade, with a significant amount of global shipping passing through the region. Both countries have demonstrated a shared interest in preserving freedom of navigation, ensuring the security of sea lanes, and combating transnational threats such as piracy, terrorism, and trafficking.

As part of India's Act East Policy, maritime cooperation has emerged as a key pillar of India-ASEAN relationship.[30] In 2018, India and Indonesia signed a pact to develop the strategic port of Sabang in Indonesia's Aceh province, located at the northern tip of Sumatra and near the Malacca Strait – one of the world's busiest shipping lanes.[31] This collaboration reflects their commitment to enhancing maritime connectivity and addressing shared security concerns in the region.

Within the broader ASEAN context, India and Indonesia both participate in several ASEAN-led mechanisms such as the ASEAN Regional Forum (ARF), the East Asia Summit (EAS), and the ASEAN Defence Ministers' Meeting Plus (ADMM-Plus). These platforms facilitate dialogues on key security issues, including counterterrorism, cyber threats, and disaster management. India and Indonesia also share concerns about China's growing assertiveness in the South China Sea, and both countries have supported efforts to uphold the rule of international law in maritime disputes.

The two countries have participated in joint naval exercises, such as the India-Indonesia Coordinated Patrol (CORPAT) and the Indian Ocean Naval Symposium (IONS), aimed at enhancing maritime security and countering piracy in the region.[32] Additionally, India and Indonesia are working together to promote infrastructure development and connectivity in the Indo-Pacific, including initiatives such as the Asia-Africa Growth Corridor (AAGC).

The convergence of India's Act East Policy and Indonesia's Global Maritime Fulcrum vision pave the way for greater strategic cooperation between the two countries in the Indo-Pacific.[33] Both Delhi and Jakarta view the Indo-Pacific as a critical space for maintaining regional stability, and they share concerns about rising tensions, particularly in the South China Sea. Through ASEAN and IORA, India and Indonesia have reaffirmed their commitment to a free, open, and inclusive Indo-Pacific.

The Indo-Pacific region is increasingly becoming a theatre of geopolitical competition, with major powers like China and the United States seeking to expand their influence. Both India and Indonesia have sought to maintain strategic autonomy and avoid entanglement in great power rivalries. However, their participation in regional institutions like ASEAN and IORA enables them to pursue a multilateral approach to address regional challenges.

By working through ASEAN and IORA, India and Indonesia can shape the rules-based order in the Indo-Pacific, promoting dialogue and cooperation over confrontation. Regional institutions provide a buffer against unilateralism and enable smaller countries to have a voice in regional decision-making.

In conclusion, India-Indonesia partnership reflects the broader goals of regional stability, economic integration, and shared security. As two leading voices in Asia, India and Indonesia's cooperation in ASEAN holds the promise of advancing the region's collective interests while fostering greater connectivity and prosperity.

NOTES

1 Mishra, Rahul (2015), "G-20: Role of India and Indonesia", in Bhatia, Rajiv and Mishra, Rahul (2015), *The Peacock and the Garuda: An Overview of India-Indonesia Relations* (New Delhi: Knowledge World)

2 Mishra, Rahul (2011), "Mosaics of Cultures: Investigating the Role of Cultural Linkages in India- Indonesia Relations", *IDSA Issue Brief,* January 19, 2011 *https://www.idsa.in/system/files/IB_IndiaIndonesia.pdf*

3 SarDesai, D. R. (1997), *Southeast Asia: Past and Present* (London: Macmillan Education UK), https://doi.org/10.1007/978-1-349-25510-8.

4 Hall, DGE (1950), *A History of South-East Asia* (London: Macmillan and Co. Ltd.).

5 For more details, see Mishra, Rahul (2011), "Mosaics of Cultures: Investigating the Role of Cultural Linkages in India- Indonesia Relations", *IDSA Issue Brief,* January 19, 2011 *https://www.idsa.in/system/files/IB_IndiaIndonesia.pdf*

6 Mahaseth, Harsh (2024), 'The Geopolitical Influence of India And Indonesia in SAARC and ASEAN', *E-International Relations* (blog), 8 September 2024, https://www.e-ir.info/2024/09/08/the-geopolitical-influence-of-india-and-indonesia-in-saarc-and-asean/.

7 Haidar, Suhasini (2023), 'How Is the Indian Ocean Rim Association a Key Bloc for India? | Explained', *The Hindu*, 14 October 2023, sec. India, https://www.thehindu.com/news/national/how-is-the-indian-ocean-rim-association-a-key-bloc-for-india-explained/article67421544.ece.

8 Muni, S D and Mishra, Rahul (2019), *India's Eastward Engagement* (New Delhi: SAGE).

9 Parmeswaran, Prashanth (2014), 'Modi Unveils India's "Act East Policy" to ASEAN in Myanmar – The Diplomat', The Diplomat, 17 November 2014, https://thediplomat.com/2014/11/modi-unveils-indias-act-east-policy-to-asean-in-myanmar/.

10 Muni and Mishra, *India's Eastward Engagement.*

11 Nabbs-Keller, Greta (2020), 'ASEAN Centrality and Indonesian Leadership in a Contested Indo-Pacific Order', *Security Challenges* 16, no. 3 (2020): 21–26.

12 Royandoyan Ramon and Damyanti, Ismi (2024), 'ASEAN Ministers Seek Myanmar Breakthrough with "troika" Model - Nikkei Asia', accessed 8 October 2024, https://asia.nikkei.com/Spotlight/Myanmar-Crisis/ASEAN-ministers-seek-Myanmar-breakthrough-with-troika-model; Devirupa Mitra, 'India, Indonesia Discuss South China Sea', The New Indian Express, 28 July 2012, https://www.newindianexpress.com/nation/2012/Jul/28/india-indonesia-discuss-south-china-sea-391413.html.

13 Mishra, Rahul (2019), 'Why India pulled out of the RCEP free trade deal', *Deutsche Welle*, 11 June 2019, https://www.dw.com/en/why-india-pulled-out-of-the-rcep-free-trade-deal/a-51137128

14 Haidar, 'How Is the Indian Ocean Rim Association a Key Bloc for India?'

15 'SagarMala - Ministry of Shipping, GOI, Government of India', accessed 8 October 2024, https://sagarmala.gov.in/.

16 Mishra, Rahul (2021), "Indo-Pacific Oceans' Initiative: Providing Institutional Framework to the Indo-Pacific Region", *AIC commentary,* No. 20, August 2021, https://aei.um.edu.my/img/files/AIC%20commentary%20No%2020%20August%202021%20final.pdf

17 'Maritime Safety & Security | Iora', accessed 8 October 2024, https://www.iora.int/maritime-safety-security.

18 'Maritime Safety & Security | Iora'.

19 ANI, 'India-Indonesia Bilateral Exercise "Samudra Shakti" Concludes in South China Sea', *The Hindu*, 20 May 2023, sec. India, https://www.thehindu.com/news/national/india-indonesia-bilateral-exercise-samudra-shakti-concludes-in-south-china-sea/article66873520.ece.

20 'Maritime Safety & Security | Iora'.

21 'Trade & Investment Facilitation | Iora', accessed 8 October 2024, https://www.iora.int/trade-investment-facilitation.

22 'Blue Economy | Iora', accessed 8 October 2024, https://www.iora.int/blue-economy.

23 'Disaster Risk Management | Iora', accessed 8 October 2024, https://www.iora.int/disaster-risk-management.

24 Premesha Saha, 'The Australia-India-Indonesia Trilateral Finally Takes Off', Observer Research Foundation, 4 October 2022, https://www.orfonline.org/expert-speak/the-australia-india-indonesia-trilateral-finally-takes-off.

25 Godbole, Shruti (2018), 'What about India, Indonesia, Australia: The New Trilateral?', 19 September 2018, https://www.brookings.edu/articles/what-about-india-indonesia-australia-the-new-trilateral/.

26 'India-Indonesia-Australia Trilateral Dialogue- Focal Points Meeting', Ministry of External Affairs, Government of India, 16 July 2024, https://mea.gov.in/press-releases.htm?dtl/37973/IndiaIndonesiaAustralia_Trilateral_Dialogue_Focal_Points_Meeting.

27 'India-Indonesia-Australia Trilateral Dialogue- Focal Points Meeting'.

28 'First Maritime Exercise Held between India, Australia and Indonesia', The New Indian Express, 22 September 2023, https://www.newindianexpress.com/nation/2023/Sep/22/first-maritime-exercise-held-between-india-australia-and-indonesia-2617346.html.

29 'Raksha Mantri Inaugurates Information Fusion Centre – Indian Ocean Region (IFC-IOR)', accessed 8 October 2024, https://pib.gov.in/Pressreleaseshare.aspx?PRID=1557074.

30 Muni and Mishra, *India's Eastward Engagement*.

31 Panda, Ankit (2018), 'India Makes Moves at Indonesia's Strategic Sabang Port', The Diplomat, 17 July 2018, https://thediplomat.com/2018/07/india-makes-moves-at-indonesias-strategic-sabang-port/.

32 Peri, Dinakar (2024), 'Indonesian Defence Establishment Could Benefit from India's Experience and Successes: Indian Envoy', *The Hindu*, 1 May 2024, sec. India, https://www.thehindu.com/news/national/indonesian-defence-establishment-could-benefit-from-indias-experience-and-successes-indian-envoy/article68128992.ece.

33 Laksmana, Evan (2019), 'Indonesia as "Global Maritime Fulcrum": A Post-Mortem Analysis', Asia Maritime Transparency Initiative, 8 November 2019, https://amti.csis.org/indonesia-as-global-maritime-fulcrum-a-post-mortem-analysis/.

10

Finding Convergence for and Values in Indonesia-India Cybersecurity Capacity-Building

*Mabda Haerunnisa Fajrilla Sidiq**

An adequate cybersecurity capacity is often thought of as an important prerequisite for a stable cyberspace. Such an understanding has motivated many efforts in cybersecurity capacity-building, intended to enhance the capacity of targetted actors, such as state actors, to enhance their ability in mitigating risks, addressing threats and maintaining resilience within their respective cyberspaces. Dialogue on international security within the context of cyberspace has long established that capacity-building is a pivotal component of cyber diplomacy (Amazouz, 2020).

In enhancing the Indonesia-India cooperation following the 75th anniversary of their bilateral relations, advancing cybersecurity cooperation might be a viable option. In this respect, capacity-building can serve as a building block for deeper engagement in other areas of cyber cooperation. This is in line with the consensus reached under the ASEAN Regional Forum (ARF), where ASEAN and their dialogue partners, including India, have noted the importance of capacity-building as a conflict prevention measure and in developing trust and confidence between members of the ARF (ARF, 2018). However, on a bilateral basis, prominent exchanges or collective activities in cyber cooperation, let alone capacity-building, is yet to materialise.

The lack of cooperation in this area is reasonable. Across various indices, Indonesia and India tend to display similar performances and are ranked similarly with other developing countries with growing digital markets. One

*Mabda Haerunnisa Fajrilla Sidiq is an Associate Fellow and Researcher, The Habibie Center.

of the primary examples is the scores achieved in the National Cybersecurity Index (NCSI), released by the e-Governance Academy in Estonia. India and Indonesia respectively received the scores of 67.53 and 63.64, where they rank 36th and 49th out of the 177 surveyed countries/territories ("NCSI-Ranking: Archived data from 01.09.2023," 2023). These scores indicate the preparedness of the surveyed countries in addressing cyber threats. The MIT Cyber Defense Index also points to a similar yet more worrying conclusion; India and Indonesia are respectively ranked in the 17th and 20th positions out of the 20 surveyed "major economies", achieving scores of 4.87 and 3.46. This indicates that both countries still have a relatively low degree of adaptability to measures in ensuring resilience from cyberattacks ("The Cyber Defense Index 2022/23," n.d.).

While Indonesia and India's performances in both indices might be deemed as worrying, it is nonetheless important to note that both countries have stepped up their commitments to enhance their respective cybersecurity capacities. The NCSI pairs its cybersecurity assessment with a measurement of digital development level; when digital development is accounted for, both countries are found to have been successful in ensuring the adequate development of cybersecurity within their respective geographical boundaries. This is proven by their comparatively higher scores in cybersecurity than digital development ("NCSI::Ranking", 2023). That aside, the International Telecommunication Union's (ITU) Global Cybersecurity Index (GCI), which measures the level of cybersecurity commitment of surveyed countries, also points to India and Indonesia's successes in showcasing strong commitments for "coordinated and government-driven actions" in securing their respective cyberspaces. Each respectively attained scores of 97.49 and 100 in the latest edition of the index (ITU, 2024).

A conventional reading to cybersecurity capacity-building would declare that both Indonesia and India are not fit for bilateral engagement in cybersecurity capacity-building. Capacity-building programmes are often thought to mirror the typical donor-recipient, North-South, developed-developing mold commonly found in traditional international development programmes (see Homburger, 2019; Collet, 2021). This form of exchange, while constructive, is not the sole model of cybersecurity capacity-building programme that states can opt for. Instead of conceiving capacity-building as a unidirectional engagement, where each actor takes the role of the "giver" or "taker," it can also be useful to find value in engagements which are multidirectional, multistakeholder, and mutually constructive in nature (see Collett, 2021). This way, it would be possible to comprehend ways cybersecurity capacity-building between developing countries, notwithstanding their progress in economic development, can still be mutually beneficial. It would thus be possible to consider capacity-building initiatives as potential building blocks for future Indonesia-India cyber cooperation.

Prior to considering Indonesia-India cooperation in cybersecurity capacity-building, I turn to recent developments in cybersecurity capacity-building to situate Indonesia and India within the ongoing debates on this issue.

Current Developments in Global Cybersecurity Capacity-Building

Discussions under the purview of the United Nations General Assembly (UNGA)-mandated UN Group of Governmental Experts on Developments in the Field of Information and Telecommunications in the Context of International Security (UNGGE) has long established the interlinkage between cybersecurity capacity-building with an international ecosystem conducive for a stable cyberspace (Amazouz, 2020). Formerly the primary UN-level channel to discuss cybersecurity, promoting cybersecurity capacity-building had long found a strong resonance within the grouping, particularly in providing support for developing countries in enhancing their technical, legal and bureaucratic capacities. The last UNGGE report, published in 2021 as a culmination of discussions taking place in 2019-2021, prescribed capacity-building actions in areas such as national policymaking, creating/enhancing/strengthening Computer Emergency Response Teams (CERTs), protection of critical infrastructure, detection/investigation/resolution of cyber incidents, application of international law in cyberspace and implementation of norms of responsible state behaviour (UNGA, 2021).

The UNGGE recommended voluntary actions from states to take initiatives in said areas, particularly under the remit of international and/or regional frameworks. Moreover, the UNGGE processes also recommended the involvement of other stakeholders in enhancing the capacity of state actors in ensuring responsible behaviors in cyberspace (UNGA, 2010, 2013, 2015). While most reports agreed under the UNGGE processes typically assumed that capacity-building would flow unidirectionally from developed to developing countries, the 2015 report noted that "capacity-building involves more than a transfer of knowledge and skills from developed to developing States," pointing to the possibility that learning process can go both ways (UNGA, 2015: 11).

Alongside processes undertaken within the UNGGE process, efforts to promote cybersecurity capacity-building have also taken place in other multilateral and multistakeholder organisations. They have also served as important avenues for defining and subsequently facilitating cybersecurity capacity-building initiatives. For instance, the Association of Southeast Asia Nations (ASEAN), of which Indonesia is a member, has ardently promoted the importance of capacity-building among its member states, which the regional organisation conceived would contribute to enhancing their "collective cybersecurity posture" and "contribute meaningfully to international discussions" (ASEAN, 2022: 12). Alternatively, another primary example would be the Global Forum on Cyber Expertise (GFCE), a multistakeholder "community" whose mission is to "strengthen cyber capacity and expertise globally" ("About GFCE", n.d.). As a member of the forum, India has immensely contributed to discussions within the GFCE community.

Discussions within the UNGGE were further advanced under the Open-Ended Working Group (OEWG) mechanism, which was first convened in 2019-2021, alongside the last iteration of the UNGGE. The UNGGE process is heavily state-centric, and, only representatives from 25 states can participate on the basis of regional representation. Meanwhile, the Russia-sponsored OEWG process is seemingly more inclusive as any state is free to participate on a voluntary basis. Besides, non-state actors such as private corporations and think tanks can also participate in the OEWG. However, various observations assert that the OEWG process was developed to undermine normative developments which had progressed under the UNGGE (Basu, et al., 2021; Lewis, 2024).

The previous OEWG process, which concluded in 2021, agreed on three principles which would guide capacity-building initiatives: process and purpose, partnerships and people. Adhering to the first principle (process and purpose) would entail ensuring that sustainability, clarity in purpose, neutrality, unconditionality, sovereignty and opportunity to access relevant technologies would underpin capacity-building efforts. Meanwhile, the second principle (partnerships) emphasized that such initiatives should be contextual, needs and demand-based, as well as recognise "national ownership." Lastly, the "people" principle underscores the importance of respecting "human rights and fundamental freedoms, be gender sensitive and inclusive, universal and non-discriminatory" (UNGA, 2021: 8).

The OEWG process for 2021-2025 is currently underway, and has further advanced discussions on cybersecurity capacity-building. While discussions are still ongoing, at the time of writing, the OEWG has thus far met for eight substantive sessions and two informal intersessional consultations. Several points of contention can be noted.

First, discussions on funding have been among the most contested, particularly with regards to the possibility of developing a trust fund to facilitate capacity-building initiatives. While supporters of this proposal assert that such a mechanism would ensure consistency in financing, other states are concerned with the possibility of redundancies and inefficiencies with existing mechanisms ("UN Open-ended Working Group (OEWG)", n.d.). The eighth substantive session resulted in most participants agreeing on setting up a voluntary trust fund under the UN (GIP Digital Watch Observatory, 2024).

The second issue pertains to the mechanism for consolidating the plethora of capacity-building initiatives by developing a Global Cyber Security Cooperation Portal, which was proposed by India (Permanent Mission of India New York, 2021). Similar to the previous issue, participants are divided due to possibilities of overlaps with similar platforms, while other participants assert that such a platform would be necessary to identify gaps within existing initiatives and the needs of participants' vis-à-vis capacity-building initiatives. In this case, India suggested that synergising the proposed portal with other precedents should be promoted (Gavriloviæ, et al., 2023). The last substantive session has agreed on providing details on ways to ensure that there would be no overlap with existing initiatives and underscoring the pivotal role of non-state stakeholders in capacity-building activities (GIP Digital Watch Observatory, 2024).

Another important issue corresponds with the extent to which capacity-building initiatives can be contextualised to their intended beneficiaries. On one hand, a uniformed approach is advocated to ensure equity. However, developing states primarily affirm that a tailored, needs-based approach would be needed to ensure that capacity-building activities would effectively address concerns and gaps found within their respective national contexts ("UN Open-ended Working Group (OEWG)", n.d.).

Lastly, another important debate is concerned with ways that gender-sensitive and inclusive approaches are taken in capacity-building. The debate centers around whether this matter is actually relevant with the OEWG's remit, given its focus on cybersecurity ("UN Open-ended Working Group (OEWG)", n.d.). Indonesia is among the countries supporting considerations for gender perspectives in the OEWG's discussion on capacity-building (Gavriloviæ, et al., 2023).

While cybersecurity capacity-building has been discussed for the last 20 years, it remains a contested form of cooperation nonetheless, particularly if one looks at existing developments in multilateral dialogues. The OEWG process will be concluded in 2025 and international discussions on cybersecurity will subsequently continue under the Programme of Action (PoA) for advancing responsible state behaviour in cyberspace. The PoA will permanently serve as the primary UN forum to discuss cyber issues in international security (see "Working paper for a Programme of Action (PoA) to advance responsible State behavior in the use of ICTs in the context of international security", 2021). While India voted in favour of the PoA mechanism, Indonesia opted to abstain. Nonetheless, a resolution to adopt the PoA mechanism was passed (GIP Digital Watch Observatory, 2022).

Amidst ongoing debates on cybersecurity capacity-building, there are multiple ways that Indonesia and India can foster and enhance engagements in cyber cooperation through capacity-building. This would particularly be relevant if one considers the value of advancing developing-developing/South-South capacity-building initiatives.

Developing-Developing/South-South Cybersecurity Capacity-Building Initiatives

Discussions on cybersecurity capacity-building have asserted that there is no need to follow the typical donor-recipient model displayed by conventional development projects. This is also asserted by various scholars, viewing that the traditional model offered by discussions on international development would limit the type of knowledge that capacity-building initiatives can transmit to participants (see Homburger, 2019).

It is necessary to address ideational barriers instilled by the traditional donor-recipient relationship in other areas of international development. Two findings might alleviate such barriers. First, scholars have found that the categorisation of states considered as "donors" or "recipients" in cybersecurity capacity-building do not necessarily have to fit into the traditional dichotomy between "developed" and "developing" economies. Digital and scientific development, rather than economic development, might serve as the primary metric in considering whether states can contribute to capacity-building by providing knowledge and know-hows (Homburger, 2019; Calderaro & Craig, 2020). While Indonesia and India are not necessarily among the most digitally advanced countries, both states have shown commendable commitment towards cybersecurity, as demonstrated by their achievements in the ITU's GCI. This points to the valuable insights that both countries might offer to each other and, potentially, other developing countries in working around limitations within their respective digital sectors.

Second, engagement between developing countries would put both actors on a level playing field, where a multidirectional flow of knowledge between participants' is more likely to take place (Collett, 2021). This would address a prevalent concern raised by various scholars on the possibility of donor countries making use of cybersecurity capacity-building initiatives as a leverage or tool to transmit certain political values to recipient countries in an environment of geopolitical rivalry (Pawlak & Barmpaliou, 2017; Homburger, 2019). This would also allow participants' to tailor their respective t capacity-building initiatives to the demands of their own locales.

Mapping Out Potential Pathways for Indonesia-India Cooperation in Cybersecurity Capacity-Building

The considerations above can serve as a basis for future Indonesia-India cooperation in cybersecurity capacity-building. I, therefore, contend that there are at least three values that future Indonesia-India cooperation in cybersecurity cooperation can consider, particularly with respect to cybersecurity capacity-building.

First, complementarity should serve as a prerequisite for future Indonesia-India cybersecurity capacity-building initiatives. Ensuring complementarity would mean that such initiatives would make use of each other's strengths to address shortcomings and comprehend the best way to learn and move forward. Complementarity would also help to ensure that these initiatives will be needs-based.

Second, both countries should also emphasize equity, meaning that bilateral cybersecurity capacity-building initiatives should mutually benefit both and prevent their interests from being jeopardised. This would allow for both countries to engage on an equal footing. Another extension of this value is emphasizing that cybersecurity capacity-building between Indonesia and India is primarily driven by the need to ensure that their respective capacities are enough to bridge existing gaps with other countries in contributing to a stable, open and peaceful cyberspace.

Third, cybersecurity capacity-building initiatives between both countries should also be proactive. On the one hand, pro-activeness can be upheld within the context of their bilateral engagement. Both countries, as best as they can, should be proactive in ensuring that cybersecurity capacity-building addresses their specific contexts and meets needs associated with such initiatives, such as funding and active participation from respective stakeholders. On the other hand, pro-activeness can be external. As two of the world's major economies, with both having global and regional standing, Indonesia and India's engagement in this area can serve as an exemplary model for other developing countries.

By adhering to the above three values, Indonesia and India can foster future engagement through cybersecurity capacity-building in several potential areas. Both parties may look at their respective strengths and weaknesses, and subsequently map out areas where mutual learning would be most beneficial. Engagement will not only be useful in developing respective capacities, but also contribute to an understanding and exemplary practice for developing countries in the Global South in a variety of ways. Developing countries can contribute to global discussions on cybersecurity capacity-building.

REFERENCES

"About GFCE." (n.d.). *GFCE.* https://thegfce.org/about-gfce/

"NCSI:: Ranking: Archived data from 01.09.2023." (2023). *NCSI.* https://ncsi.ega.ee/ncsi-index/?archive=1

"The Cyber Defense Index 2022/23." (n.d.). *MIT Technology Review.* https://www.technologyreview.com/2022/11/15/1063189/the-cyber-defense-index-2022-23/

"UN Open-ended Working Group (OEWG)." (n.d.). *dig.watch.* Retrieved from 12 September 2024. https://dig.watch/processes/un-gge#Unresolved-issues

"Working paper for a Programme of Action (PoA) to advance responsible State behavior in the use of ICTs in the context of international security." (2021). https://documents.unoda.org/wp-content/uploads/2021/11/Working-paper-on-the-proposal-for-a-Cyber-PoA.pdf

Amazouz, S. (2020). Cyber Capacity-Building and International Security. In E. Tikk & M. Kerttunen (Eds.). *Routledge Handbook of International Cybersecurity* (p. 201-213). Routledge.

ARF. (2018). ASEAN REGIONAL FORUM STATEMENT ON COOPERATION IN THE FIELD OF SECURITY OF AND IN THE USE OF ICTS IN THE CONTEXT OF INTERNATIONAL SECURITY. https://aseanregionalforum.asean.org/wp-content/uploads/2020/09/ADOPTED_ARF-Statement-on-Cooperation-in-the-Field-of-Security-of-and-in-the-Use-of-ICTs-in-the-Context-of-International-Security.pdf

ASEAN. (2022). *ASEAN CYBERSECURITY COOPERATION STRATEGY (2021-2025).* https://asean.org/wp-content/uploads/2022/02/01-ASEAN-Cybersecurity-Cooperation-Paper-2021-2025_final-23-0122.pdf

Basu, A., Poetranto, I., & Lau, J. (2021, May 19). The UN Struggles to Make Progress on Securing Cyberspace. *Carnegie Endowment for International Peace.* https://carnegieendowment.org/research/2021/05/the-un-struggles-to-make-progress-on-securing-cyberspace?lang=en

Calderaro, A. & Craig, A.J.S. (2020). Transnational governance of cybersecurity: policy challenges and global inequalities in cyber capacity building. *Third World Quarterly.* https://doi.org/10.1080/01436597.2020.1729729

Collett, R. (2021). Understanding cybersecurity capacity building and its relationship to norms and confidence building measures. *Journal of Cyber Policy, 6*(3): 298-317. https://doi.org/10.1080/23738871.2021.1948582

Gavriloviæ, A., Kazakova, A., Ittelson, P., Stadnik, I., & Siemens, S.P. (2023). "OEWG's sixth substantive session: the highlights." *dig.watch.* https://dig.watch/updates/oewgs-sixth-substantive-session-the-highlights

GIP Digital Watch Observatory. (2022, November 3). Resolution on the programme of action (PoA) on cybersecurity adopted. *dig.watch.* https://dig.watch/updates/resolution-on-the-programme-of-action-poa-on-cybersecurity-adopted

GIP Digital Watch Observatory. (2024, July 30). OEWG's eighth substantive session: third progress report adopted, what's next for ICT discussions? *dig.watch.* https://dig.watch/updates/oewgs-eighth-substantive-session-the-highlights

Homburger, Z. (2019). The Necessity and Pitfall of Cybersecurity Capacity Building for Norm Development in Cyberspace. *Global Society, 33*(2): 224-242. https://doi.org/10.1080/13600826.2019.1569502

ITU. (2024). *Global Cybersecurity Index 2024 (5th Edition).*

Lewis, J.A. (2024, July 16). Why the United Nations Is Chasing Its Tail on Cybersecurity. *CSIS.* https://www.csis.org/analysis/why-united-nations-chasing-its-tail-cybersecurity

Pawlak, P. & Barmpaliou, P-N. (2017). Politics of cybersecurity capacity building: conundrum and opportunity. *Journal of Cyber Policy*. https://doi.org/10.1080/23738871.2017.1294610

Permanent Mission of India New York. (2021). *Working Paper on Global Cyber Security Cooperation Portal*. https://docs-library.unoda.org/Open-Ended_Working_Group_on_ Information _ and _ Communication_Technologies_-_(2021)/WP_GCSCP.pdf

UNGA. (2010). *Report of the Group of Governmental Experts on Developments in the Field of Information and Telecommunications in the Context of International Security*. A/65/201. https://documents.un.org/doc/undoc/gen/n10/469/57/pdf/n1046957.pdf

UNGA. (2013). *Report of the Group of Governmental Experts on Developments in the Field of Information and Telecommunications in the Context of International Security*. A/68/98. https://digitallibrary.un.org/nanna/record/753055/files/A_68_98-EN.pdf?withWatermark= 0&withMetadata=0&version=1®isterDownload=1

UNGA. (2015). *Report of the Group of Governmental Experts on Developments in the Field of Information and Telecommunications in the Context of International Security*. A/70/174. https://documents.un.org/doc/undoc/gen/n15/228/35/pdf/n1522835.pdf

UNGA. (2021a). *Report of the Group of Governmental Experts on Advancing Responsible State Behaviour in Cyberspace in the Context of International Security*. A/76/135. https://front.un-arm.org/wp-content/uploads/2021/08/A_76_135-2104030E-1.pdf

UNGA. (2021b). *Open-ended working group on developments in the field of information and telecommunications in the context of international security: Final Substantive Report*. A/AC.290/2021/CRP.2. https://front.un-arm.org/wp-content/uploads/2021/03/Final-report-A-AC.290-2021-CRP.2.pdf

11

Beyond Bilateralism: Strengthening India-Indonesia Ties within ASEAN

Dr Cchavi Vasisht

Introduction

The India-ASEAN relationship has evolved significantly over the past three decades, deepening in various areas of cooperation. Initially a Sectoral Dialogue Partner in 1992, India's engagement with ASEAN has grown steadily, culminating in the formation of a Comprehensive Strategic Partnership in 2022. Throughout this period, both have expanded cooperation in areas, including, socio-cultural, economic and political-security. While India's engagement with individual Southeast Asian nations has varied over time, its interactions with Singapore, Malaysia, Vietnam and Indonesia have been particularly noteworthy. For this article, we will focus on India's relations with Indonesia whose leadership in fostering India-ASEAN relations has been noteworthy. This article attempts to explore the India-Indonesia ties, especially within the ASEAN Framework. Indonesia is a founding member of ASEAN and its contributions to ASEAN include creating agreements, participating in peace efforts and maintaining regional security.

Mechanisms for India-ASEAN Cooperation

India's engagement with ASEAN has focussed on three main objectives: (i) boosting connectivity with ASEAN across various dimensions, including physical, digital, people-to-people, and business linkages; (ii) reinforcing the

*Dr Cchavi Vasisht is a Senior Research Associate, Chintan Research Foundation, Delhi.

strength and cohesion of the ASEAN organisation; and (iii) expanding collaboration in the maritime sector. The India-ASEAN relationship is characterised by a multi-layered engagement process involving various mechanisms at different levels. These mechanisms facilitate cooperation and dialogue between the two in many sectors. The key mechanisms for engagement include the annual ASEAN-India Summits which are the highest forum for bilateral engagement. It provides an opportunity for leaders to discuss issues and chart the future course of the relationship. The ASEAN-India Foreign Ministers Meeting (AIFMM) serves as a platform for discussing political and diplomatic issues. The ASEAN-India Senior Officials Meeting (AISOM) and the ASEAN-India Joint Cooperation Committee (AIJCC) is a forum to discuss technical and operational matters.

India further engages with ASEAN through sectoral dialogues such as the ASEAN Economic Ministers-India Consultations (AEM +India), the ASEAN-India Ministerial Meeting on Agriculture and Forestry (AIMMAF) and the ASEAN-India Working Group on Science and Technology (AIWGST) and many others. India also participates in ASEAN-led frameworks such as the East Asia Summit (EAS), the ASEAN Regional Forum (ARF) and the Expanded ASEAN Maritime Forum (EAMF). Cooperation between India and ASEAN is facilitated through plans such as the five-year Plan of Action, or the work plans developed during interactions with ASEAN sectoral bodies. India supports these activities via three funds, namely, the ASEAN-India Cooperation Fund (AIF), the ASEAN-India Green Fund (AIGF) and the ASEAN-India Science and Technology Development Fund (AISTDF).

There is also a Track 1.5 mechanism named the "Delhi Dialogue" that brings together government officials, academics and civil society representatives from India and ASEAN to discuss issues related to the partnership. Apart from these interactions, there is a dedicated institution named the ASEAN-India Centre that supports cooperation and dialogue between India and ASEAN. All of these mechanisms provide India and ASEAN an opportunity to engage on political, economic, security and cultural cooperation issues, besides others. Through them, both sides have been able to build trust, strengthen ties and promote cooperation with each other. In 2022, the ASEAN and India forged the ASEAN-India Comprehensive Strategic Partnership (CSP) and celebrated the 30th anniversary of ASEAN-India relations.[1] Cooperation between ASEAN and India has steadily grown in the areas of culture, social development, economic and political-security.[2] The details of this are outlined in the latest Plan of Action to Implement the ASEAN-India Partnership for Peace, Progress and Shared Prosperity (2021-2025)[3]. Looking ahead, ASEAN and India have the potential to make significant contributions to regional peace, stability and prosperity. Areas in focus include sustainable development, climate change and maritime security. In the sphere of political-security, the plan of action includes continuing dialogue in various platforms, maritime cooperation and collaboration to combat transnational crime and terrorism. Towards this, ASEAN and India continue to hold the "Delhi Dialogue". India recently also hosted the ASEAN Inter-Parliamentary Assembly (AIPA) delegation.

Here, it would be useful to focus on a key India-ASEAN objective, i.e., expanding maritime sector collaboration. India's maritime engagement with the ASEAN has culminated in the first-ever ASEAN-India maritime exercise in May 2023. It reflects India's growing emphasis on the need for maritime cooperation with Southeast Asia, driven by strategic interests, security concerns and regional dynamics.

In the early 1990s, India's engagement with ASEAN focussed on bilateral and multilateral dialogues and economic initiatives even as India was in the midst of economic reforms. Over time, as maritime security gained global prominence, particularly during China's rise and increasing territorial disputes over the South China Sea, India began expanding its maritime collaboration with ASEAN states. India already had bilateral naval exercises with individual ASEAN nations, as well as a trilateral exercise with Singapore and Thailand. However, the formalisation of collective maritime cooperation with ASEAN was a major leap.

The 2023 ASEAN-India Maritime Exercise has to be seen as a watershed moment in India's maritime engagement with Southeast Asia. Hosted by Singapore, the exercise brought together the navies of India and several ASEAN nations to strengthen maritime security collaboration. It highlighted India's readiness to work collectively with ASEAN in securing the Indo-Pacific region, a key maritime zone for global trade and geopolitical stability.

Beyond Bilateralism: India-Indonesia Maritime Cooperation

India-Indonesia relations have been shaped by geographic proximity, cultural similarities and shared anti-colonial and non-aligned ideals, as seen in their joint leadership at the 1955 Bandung Conference. However, differences over the Non-Aligned Movement and China led to a drift in ties, which was further strained during the Cold War. Nonetheless, relations improved in the late 20th century with Indian Prime Minister Rajiv Gandhi's visit to Jakarta in 1986 and gained momentum after the Cold War, particularly with India's "Look East" policy in 1991. India-Indonesia relations matured, marked by growing economic, trade and defence cooperation, including the 2001 Defense Cooperation Agreement and the 2005 Comprehensive Strategic Partnership Agreement. It was during this time that India also became an ASEAN Sectoral Dialogue Partner in 1992.

An area that has been of keen interest to both nations is maritime cooperation as both have shared concerns about maritime security, piracy and the South China Sea dispute, and thereby positioned themselves as potential maritime partners in the Indo-Pacific region.[4] Back in 1958, both countries signed a naval security agreement, followed by their first joint naval exercise in 1960. During the Cold War, both worked together to limit the Western influence in the Indian Ocean, co-sponsoring the Indian Ocean Zone of Peace proposal. Bilateral naval exercises continued through the 1980s and 1990s, with coordinated patrols in the Straits of Malacca since 2002. Indonesia has also participated in the India-led multilateral naval exercises like MILAN and SAREX.

In recent years, Indonesia's President Joko Widodo's vision of a "Global Maritime Fulcrum" (GMF) aligns with India's own maritime aspirations. In 2018, India and Indonesia signed a "Shared Vision for Maritime Cooperation in the Indo-Pacific," outlining their shared goals and priorities for cooperation in the maritime domain.[5] The two countries have continued to strengthen their naval cooperation through joint exercises, information sharing and capacity building. They have also explored opportunities for cooperation in the maritime sector, such as port development and maritime infrastructure.[6] The Trilateral Dialogue on the Indian Ocean (TDIO) between India, Indonesia and Australia, and the Indian Ocean Rim Association (IORA), provide further platforms for cooperation.

Furthermore, Indonesia, as the largest economy and most populous country in ASEAN, plays a pivotal role in shaping the regional landscape.[7] Its significance for India's Act East Policy is manifold, especially acting as an economic gateway and maritime security partner. Indonesia serves as a gateway to the vast market, offering immense potential for Indian businesses in sectors such as pharmaceuticals, information technology and automobiles. Moreover, Indonesia's strategic location can facilitate Indian trade and investment with the other ASEAN countries. Both India and Indonesia face similar security challenges, including terrorism, maritime security and climate change. Strong bilateral cooperation in these areas can enhance regional stability and address shared threats. Finally, Indonesia's leadership within ASEAN is undeniable. In addition to the above bilateral cooperation, Indonesia has fostered India-ASEAN maritime relations under its leadership.

During its ASEAN chairmanship in 2023, Indonesia played a pivotal role in strengthening cooperation between both sides.[8] In addition to a joint statement on food security, Indonesia championed a joint statement on maritime cooperation, highlighting the importance of maintaining peace and stability in the region. The ASEAN-India Joint Statement on Maritime Cooperation outlined a comprehensive framework for cooperation in various maritime sectors, reflecting the shared interests and goals of both entities in promoting peace, stability, and prosperity in the Indo-Pacific region. The key areas of cooperation under the Joint Statement include,

- **Maritime Safety and Security:** Enhancing information sharing, capacity building and cooperation in areas such as search and rescue, pollution control and combating maritime crimes.
- **Sustainable Development of Marine Resources:** Promoting responsible fishing practices, combating illegal, unregulated, unreported fishing and protecting marine environments.
- **Trade and Investment:** Enhancing connectivity, promoting trade and investment flows, and developing maritime infrastructure.
- **Blue Economy:** Promoting the sustainable development of marine resources and exploring new economic opportunities in the maritime sector.
- **Science and Technology:** Enhancing cooperation in marine science, technology and innovation.

- **Humanitarian Assistance and Disaster Relief (HADR):** Strengthening disaster preparedness, response and recovery efforts.

The Joint Statement provides a solid foundation for India-ASEAN cooperation in the maritime domain.[9] By working together, India and ASEAN can make significant contributions to the peace, stability, and prosperity of the Indo-Pacific region. Indonesia has also proposed a framework to formalise the ASEAN-IORA cooperation, aiming to build an inclusive regional architecture and has sought India's support for this framework.

However, there are challenges which have affected their relationship. With global powers like the U.S. and China revising their approach to globalisation and India's withdrawal from the Regional Comprehensive Economic Partnership (RCEP) in 2019, the ASEAN has been disappointed, particularly as India's economic presence was seen as a counterbalance to China's dominance. Additionally, the shift from the "Asia-Pacific" to the "Indo-Pacific" as a new strategic geography, particularly championed by the U.S., has created discomfort in ASEAN. Southeast Asian nations view the Indo-Pacific as closely tied to the growing geopolitical conflict between the U.S. and China, something ASEAN is cautious about navigating. Despite this, ASEAN issued its own "ASEAN Outlook on the Indo-Pacific" in 2019,[10] but the larger geopolitical implications remain unresolved. Also, the revival of the Quad (comprising India, Australia, Japan, and the U.S.) has created concerns within the ASEAN about its centrality in shaping regional security architecture. Some ASEAN members worry that the Quad might sideline ASEAN's role in promoting regional peace and stability.

Other Areas of Cooperation between India and ASEAN and Contribution of Indonesia

Apart from maritime domain cooperation, there is an ongoing cooperation in the economic and the socio-cultural sphere. On the economic front, key institutional mechanisms include the ASEAN Economic Ministers-India Consultations (AEM+India), which focuses on reviewing the ASEAN-India Trade in Goods Agreement (AITIGA), and the ASEAN-India Business Council (AIBC), which promotes private sector dialogue and partnership. Bilateral trade between India and ASEAN reached USD 110.39 billion in FY 2021-22, with exports from India amounting to USD 42.33 billion and imports from ASEAN worth USD 68.07 billion. Within this, Indonesia is India's second largest trading partner in ASEAN (first being Singapore). Recently, ASEAN and India approved the scope of the review of the ASEAN-India Trade in Goods Agreement to make it simple and user-friendly and to truncate trade transactions. Further, ASEAN's cumulative FDI in India is USD 117.88 billion between 2000 and 2021, out of which Singapore has been the dominant source of ASEAN investments in India, contributing USD 115 billion.[11] There are also many Indian companies operating in Indonesia, including IT companies, coal mining companies and manufacturing companies.

The two sides also work in the promotion of energy security through the development of renewable and alternative energy sources, and an integrated regional power grid, research and development (R&D) and capacity building in the field of science and technology, and support to digital connectivity and skills development. All this has been part of the recent Plan of Action (2021-2025). In line with this, they held a High-Level Conference on Renewable Energy to facilitate knowledge sharing on factors that impact the integrated renewables market. In science and technology, the ASEAN and India launched the inaugural ASEAN-India Start-up Festival, which aims to showcase the most promising innovations in the region. In the digital sector, several activities have been completed, or are underway, such as the Cyber Threat Hunting Webinar and the multitude of training courses on advanced satellite communication, 5G and Internet of Things, ICT in disaster management, telecommunication security, mobile communication and future trends, and cyber forensics.

The Plan of Action (2021-2025) also focuses on educational and media exchanges, capacity building of ASEAN citizens through Indian scholarships, teaching and research partnerships, promotion of women and youth participation in human development programmes, documentation and dissemination of knowledge about civilisational links between ASEAN and India, and disaster management and humanitarian assistance. Following this plan of action, ASEAN and India pursued the following programmes and activities: various scholarships for ASEAN students at Nalanda University, Doctoral Fellowship in India for ASEAN, ASEAN-India Media Exchange Visits, ASEAN-India Youth Summit, ASEAN-India Music Festival, ASEAN-India Artists' Camp, International Conference on ASEAN India Cultural and

Civilisational Links, and The ASEAN magazine. ASEAN and India likewise launched two new projects this year. One is the setting up of an expert panel and ad-hoc working group to study the feasibility of an ASEAN Cultural Heritage List. The other is the ASEAN-India Network of Universities, which gives participating universities from ASEAN and India an opportunity to form linkages in three areas: faculty exchange, doctoral student exchange and joint research or PhD research supervision.

Moving Forward: A Maritime Partnership for the Indo-Pacific

To ensure that maritime cooperation remains strong, India will need to address ASEAN's concerns over the Quad and the Indo-Pacific construct. India must reassure ASEAN that the Quad will not undermine ASEAN's central role in the region but will instead complement its efforts for regional peace and security.[12] The ASEAN-India maritime exercise is a step in this direction, showcasing India's willingness to engage ASEAN on security issues within a multilateral framework. Furthermore, expanding political consultations, intensifying defence and maritime cooperation, and ensuring that the Quad's initiatives align with ASEAN's security interests are critical for maintaining a balance. India's leadership must work to prevent strategic divergences with ASEAN.

India's journey of maritime engagement with ASEAN has grown from cautious bilateral interactions to a more comprehensive multilateral framework. While new geopolitical complexities present challenges, the first ASEAN-India maritime exercise represents a promising step in aligning India's security interests with ASEAN's goals for regional stability. It will be important for India to continue nurturing this relationship, ensuring that ASEAN's centrality is respected while enhancing maritime cooperation in the evolving Indo-Pacific context. The shared vision for maritime cooperation in the Indo-Pacific region, as outlined in the 2018 joint statement, reflects the growing convergence of interests between India and Indonesia. By continuing to work together and address these challenges, the two countries can further strengthen their partnership and contribute to the peace, stability, and prosperity of the Indo-Pacific region.

NOTES

1 https://asean.org/wp-content/uploads/2024/06/Overview-ASEAN-India-as-of-June-2024-cl.pdf

2 Key outcomes of the 19th ASEAN-India Summit included the adoption of a Joint Statement on ASEAN-India Comprehensive Strategic Partnership and an additional USD 5 million contribution to the ASEAN-India Science and Technology Development Fund (AISTDF). https://pib.gov.in/PressReleaseIframePage.aspx?PRID=1517931

3 https://asean.org/wp-content/uploads/2023/07/05_Final-ASEAN-India-PoA-with-Annex-1.pdf

4 https://maritimeindia.org/india-and-indonesia-translating-strategic-convergence-into-maritime-cooperation/

5 https://www.gatewayhouse.in/indonesian-presidents-visit-a-reluctant-ritual/

6 https://www.mea.gov.in/bilateral-documents.htm?dtl/29933/Shared_Vision_of_India Indonesia _Maritime_Cooperation_in_the_IndoPacific

7 https://www.gatewayhouse.in/indonesian-presidents-visit-a-reluctant-ritual/

8 https://kemlu.go.id/portal/en/read/6095/berita/indonesia-encouraged-asean-india-to-strengthen-food-security-and-maritime-cooperation#:~:text=For%20this%20reason%2C %20 Indonesia%20encourage,development%20of%20maritime%20energy%20resources. https://asean.org/wp-content/uploads/2023/09/FINAL-Chairmans-Statement-of-the-20th-ASEAN-India-Summit.pdf

9 https://www.mea.gov.in/Images/CPV/ASEAN-India-Joint-Statement-on-Maritime-Cooperatio_230907_160027.pdf

10 The ASEAN-India Joint Statement on Cooperation on the ASEAN Outlook on the Indo-Pacific for Peace, Stability, and Prosperity in the Region outlines a comprehensive framework for cooperation between the two entities. https://asean.org/wp-content/uploads/2021/10/71.-ASEAN-India-Joint-Statement-on-Cooperation-on-the-ASEAN-Outlook-on-the-Indo-Pacific-for-Peace-Stability-and-Prosperity-in-the-Region-Final.pdf

11 https://www.aseanbriefing.com/news/boosting-india-asean-economic-collaboration-key-highlights-from-pm-modis-12-point-proposal/

12 https://www.isas.nus.edu.sg/papers/india-asean-maritime-engagement/

12

Evolving Geopolitical Dynamics of the Indo-Pacific Region and its Impact on India-Indonesia Relations

Vinod Anand and Faisal Ahmed***

Introduction

The Indo-Pacific has been playing a key role amid global contestations in the present scenario.[1] The region has emerged as a critical area in the struggle for a new geopolitical world order. For instance, an increase in Chinese naval assertiveness has become a contentious issue in the South China Sea (SCS) region. Countries like the United States are making attempts to bolster efforts towards countering the threats posed by the increase in China's naval activities. Moreover, the SCS issue has become an area of heightened competition between a number of major powers. As countries face tough relations with China, powers such as the United States, Japan, and Australia aim to have an Indo-Pacific vision emphasising a marginal sea at one end and the oceans at the other.[2] Countries such as Indonesia, Malaysia and the Philippines have continuously sought support on the fisherman issue in the maritime territories.

Importantly, India is considered to be a significant player in the region. On the geopolitical front, India's Indo-Pacific policy has always been at the forefront of strengthening its partnerships and promoting coalitions to provide new mechanisms and frameworks for resolving strategic and security issues. India's bilateral relations with all the ASEAN members remain cordial. In this regard, India has been known for its soft power aspects linked to this region.

*Vinod Anand is a Senior Fellow, Vivekananda International Foundation.

**Dr Faisal Ahmed is a Professor of International Business and Geopolitics at FORE School of Management, New Delhi.

India strives to be a dependable and strategic security partner in the region. In 2023, it co-hosted the ASEAN-Indian maritime exercise in the South China Sea (SCS). India had fielded a number of ships, including INS Delhi and the Stealth frigate INS Satpura. Interestingly, India looks forward to growing its defence partnership with Indonesia by collaborating in many areas including in submarines; INS Sindhu Kesari, India's Kilo Class submarine had docked in Jakarta in Feb 2023 which was the first such port call to Indonesia.

Indonesia continues to grapple with its strategic challenges in the Indo-Pacific region. Over the years, it has established a strategic space for itself. This has been reflected in its foreign policy throughout the 20th century. Nevertheless, an Indonesian initiative to increase participation in different sub-regional frameworks indirectly signals the shift towards the Indo-Pacific.

Since 2007, the term "Indo-Pacific" has been consistently emphasised upon. This includes an offer for an Indo-Pacific Treaty of Friendship and Cooperation (IPTFC), to recognise Indonesia as a key maritime hub connecting Indian and the Pacific Ocean (Scott, 2019).

Indonesia's perception of the Indo-Pacific region has become closely linked to its diplomatic relations with major countries including India, China, and the United States. This includes Indonesia's response to these countries' strategies and policies. It is crucial to highlight that Indonesia has exercised restrain in expanding its influence in the Indian and Pacific Oceans. Interestingly, Scott (2019) has asserted that if seen geographically, Indonesia has been a quintessential Indo-Pacific power, facing the Indian Ocean on the west, the South China Sea on the north, and the Pacific Ocean on the east. The author further asserted that from the 1950s to the 1990s, Indonesia focussed mainly on maintaining archipelagic cohesion and regional focus on the ASEAN grouping (Association of South Eastern Asian Nations). [3]

Countries have tried to build long-term strategic orientation to secure the Indo-Pacific region. In this regard, it becomes imperative to cultivate awareness of the Free and Open Indo-Pacific (FOIP) strategy, which consists of three pillars: (a) promotion and the establishment of the rule of law, freedom of navigation and trade; (b) pursuit of economic prosperity; (c) commitment for peace and stability. [4] This move by the Japanese PM was seen as efficient. The FOIP vision laid the ground specifically for countries like India, not only for their economic development but also for the global community. This signifies that India's vision for the Indo-Pacific would enhance its geopolitical engagement with Indonesia. Both countries are aiming to enhance their interoperability in the IOR. On the strategic front, India is also collaborating with Indonesia in the development of its port infrastructure.

The Indonesian government has recognised the significance of the Indian Ocean, mainly due to its establishment of the Indian Ocean Rim Association (IORA) in 1997. Nevertheless, it first maintained a discreet presence within a modest organisation. Indonesia is expanding beyond ASEAN and is now venturing into the broader Indo-Pacific region. In this process, Indonesia is actively establishing significant bilateral connections with China, Australia, India, Japan, and the United States.[5] Agastia (2020) contends that Indonesia's foreign policymakers have significantly emphasised analysing their nation's strategic geographic position between the Indian and Pacific Oceans. The author asserts that there have been restricted and targetted endeavours to cultivate the Indonesian notion of the Indo-Pacific region. Indonesia emphasises showcasing its close geographical connection to Southeast Asia. It is essential to understand that Indonesia's viewpoint on the Indo-Pacific is comprehensive and unified, with no aim of excluding any stakeholder. The ASEAN Outlook on the Indo-Pacific (AOIP) has recognised Indonesia's ambition (Anwar, 2020). The AOIP advocates for the interconnected and integrated nature of the Indo-Pacific region and has no objective of creating new frameworks in this regard. Furthermore, it highlights the importance of inclusivity in the ideas and recommendations, signalling to other participants that ASEAN aims to maintain its prominent role despite differing perspectives on the Indo-Pacific (Weatherbee, 2019).

Furthermore, as the nations were striving to collaborate and cooperate to have a more robust agenda for the Indo-Pacific region, the year 2022 saw the formation of the Indo-Pacific Economic Framework for Prosperity (IPEF) by the United States. The members of the IPEF include Australia, Brunei Darussalam, Fiji, India, Indonesia, Japan, Korea, Malaysia, New Zealand, Philippines, Singapore, Thailand and Vietnam. The IPEF emphasises different parameters that aim to advance the issues of sustainability, inclusivity, economic growth, and competitiveness of the economies. Regarding Indonesia's role, it may be interesting to note that Indonesia's support for the IPEF is premised on the likelihood of making significant gains in market access to the United States as there is no free trade agreement between them.

Interestingly, with the opening of IPEF, Indonesia saw an exciting opportunity to deepen its engagement with the United States. The support for IPEF reflects a like-minded approach to relations between Indonesia and the United States. This was very evident in the year 2023 when the presidents of both countries advanced their relationship to a comprehensive partnership.[6] Therefore, Indonesia's support for the IPEF is crucial to keeping itself aligned with the ASEAN aims and visions. Indonesia has always envisioned fostering regional integration within the ASEAN.

China's Orientation Towards the Indonesia-led Indo-Pacific

China has embraced ASEAN's Indonesia-led Indo-Pacific perspective because it is inclusive and promotes unity (Anya, 2018).[7] Chinese Foreign Minister Wang Yi had a positive response in a news release in July 2019. The Foreign Minister acknowledged China's current cooperation agreements with ASEAN and highlighted China's receptive and constructive approach towards the Indonesia-led AOIP. The Minister also recognised that many of the principles outlined in the Outlook align with China's expectations. On the other hand, the United States emphasises the concept of ASEAN centrality in the AOIP. The US Mission to ASEAN approved the AOIP in a press statement, highlighting its significance in demonstrating ASEAN unity and acknowledging its alignment with the US Free and Open Indo-Pacific agenda (US Mission to ASEAN, 2019). [8]

In fact, the maritime fulcrum that the Indonesian foreign policy entails comprise a fivefold agenda, which includes (1) fostering a maritime culture, (2) enhancing the management of Indonesia's oceans and fisheries to strengthen maritime "food sovereignty," (3) improving the country's port infrastructure and shipping industry to boost Indonesia's maritime economy, (4) strengthening Indonesia's maritime defence to achieve maritime sovereignty and security, and (5) expanding diplomacy. Issues two to four pertain to Indonesia's strategic position at the centre of the Indo-Pacific region, which is of significant importance in traditional geopolitics. Indonesia is also a crucial transit point between the Indian and Pacific Oceans. On the other hand, issue five contends that Indonesia's interactions with other influential nations in the Indo-Pacific. One issue is the influence of marine culture on the formation of perspectives for a projected maritime zone, as constructed by critical geopolitics. The public announcement had an obvious significance: it established Indonesia as a prominent force in the Indo-Pacific region (Agastia & Perwita, 2015; Aufiya, 2017). Indonesia has a significant role in the geopolitical landscape as a strategic point of access and control for the Indian and Pacific oceans. It acts as a gateway and a gatekeeper, ensuring the security of Sea Lanes of Communications in the Indo-Pacific region.

Indonesia's Trade Policy

Indonesia's trade policy has been undergoing significant changes for decades. The study by Patunru and Rahardja (2015) and Patunru et al. (2018) reported that the trade policy of Indonesia as being caught between embracing openness and practising protectionism for several years, starting from the inception of the New Order regime. Recent developments indicate that this characterisation is still accurate.

Hill and Pane (2018) analyse the persistent and pervasive uncertainty around globalisation, which has led to Indonesia missing out on potential benefits such as increased job creation and poverty alleviation. Indonesia's liberalising policies in certain areas while implementing 'damaging' regulations in other sectors reflects a sense of ambivalence. In addition, as Indonesia actively seeks several trade deals, it is also adopting a more protectionist stance. Indonesia has recently collaborated with nations like Australia to ensure a steady lithium supply to develop their electric vehicle (EV) battery industry. At the same time, they have banned the export of nickel ores from Indonesia (Patunru, 2023).

The trading relationship between India and Indonesia in 2023 has demonstrated substantial trade values, with both nations exchanging diverse items. India's main exports to Indonesia are mineral fuels, cars, and machinery. Mineral fuels comprised a significant proportion of India's exports to Indonesia, accounting for almost $966 million. Additional crucial exports comprise automobiles and components, estimated at approximately $952 million, and machinery, respectively. India imports commodities such as palm oils, coal, and natural rubber from Indonesia. These imports hold substantial value, particularly palm oil, mainly fuelled by India's massive local need for edible oils. Furthermore, the trade between the two nations is distinguished by various items, demonstrating a robust and comprehensive economic partnership. Both nations are crucial trading allies in the Asia-Pacific region, and their trade activities significantly impact the region's overall economic dynamics. The report by the World Bank (2024) has also asserted that Indonesia possesses an untapped potential market for exports of green goods and plastic substitutes. It has also been stated that the imported goods from Indonesia have been at par excellence with global and regional averages. [9]

Moreover, under the European Free Trade Association, Indonesia has entered into bilateral free trade agreements (FTAs) with Australia, Chile, Mozambique, Iceland, Liechtenstein, Norway, and Switzerland. However, as of the end of 2019, none of these FTAs, save for the one with Chile, have been implemented. Indonesia and Korea has officially implemented Comprehensive Economic Partnership Agreement in January, 2023. Furthermore, Indonesia-European Free Trade Association Comprehensive Economic Partnership entered into force in November, 2021. Additionally, Indonesia is reviewing its existing trade accords with Japan and Pakistan.[10] In his study, Patunru (2023) highlighted Indonesia's exports and imports of goods from 2010 to 2023. He further demonstrates the significance of the manufacturing and mining sectors in exports while highlighting the comparatively lower significance of agriculture. Simultaneously, there was a significant rise in the proportion of coal, demonstrating the ongoing significance of this resource despite efforts to decrease Indonesia's dependence on it.

Indonesia's imports mainly comprise raw materials (intermediate goods) and capital goods. Indonesia's production is still dependent on imported content, which means that its exports are also heavily reliant on imported resources. To enhance export promotion, it is necessary to increase the availability of intermediate inputs in order to boost output. Pane and Patunru (2023) establish that the productivity of Indonesian manufacturing companies is enhanced by an augmentation in the assortment and overall worth of imported inputs. The primary advantages arise from the availability of alternative resources. The advantages are more significant when the inputs come from industrialized nations, like Japan, which provides over 15% of Indonesia's intermediate inputs. This indicates that Indonesian companies also profit from technological advancements and product quality.

Indonesia's Role in ASEAN

Following Cambodia, Indonesia assumed the chairmanship of ASEAN for the fifth time in 2023. Indonesia's accomplishments extend beyond its role as the chair of ASEAN. Indonesia remains actively engaged in various significant matters within the ASEAN area.

Indonesia is establishing political, economic, social, and cultural agreements. Indonesia has actively participated in various significant matters within ASEAN, particularly in Myanmar. During the 42nd ASEAN Summit in Labuan Bajo, Indonesia, all ASEAN member countries except Myanmar introduced the Five-Point Consensus (5PC) to assist Myanmar in resolving its political problem.[11] Indonesia was chosen as the mediator in the Philippines conflict because of its neutrality and the assumption that Indonesia comprehends the conflict between the Philippines and the Moro National Liberation Front (MNLF).

India-Indonesia Relations

Indonesia and India have a long-standing historical and cultural bond for centuries. The economic relationship between India and Indonesia has experienced remarkable expansion, particularly after 1991, when India adopted the Look East policy. India has established multiple bilateral institutional frameworks to enhance its relations with Indonesia. The commerce ministers of both nations have been regularly convening meetings since 2011. Similarly, a CEO forum has been established to investigate and capitalize on economic prospects.

India's economic relationship with Indonesia has been developed through bilateral procedures and India's increased engagement with ASEAN, of which Indonesia is a significant component. In 2000, the bilateral trade between India and Indonesia was less than US$ 3 billion. By 2010, it had expanded to US$ 14.2 billion; by 2022-23, it had risen to US$ 38.85 billion. The potential for bilateral commerce between India and Indonesia is estimated to be US$ 61 billion, approximately 33% more than the present trade volume. The trading potential encompasses various products, such as certain agricultural products, pharmaceuticals, autos, automotive components, engineering products, minerals, and metals.[12]

Digital technology, on the other hand, presents both opportunities and challenges. Both countries have made remarkable progress in deindustrialisation. India has successfully constructed digital public infrastructure, leading to enhanced delivery of public services and the emergence of numerous digital innovations. Indonesia has also successfully advanced the digitalisation of micro, small, and medium enterprises (MSMEs). Hence, a significant opportunity exists for reciprocal knowledge acquisition through exchanging experiences, which should be actively pursued.[13] Indonesia has placed a high importance on advancing its economy. Indonesia has placed utmost importance on human development.

China holds a prominent position in Indonesia. The Chinese population exerts significant dominance over the industrial sector in Indonesia. In addition, Indonesia has also welcomed significant Chinese investment through the Belt and Road initiative, which has generated a degree of apprehension. Nevertheless, the issue is more intricate than it initially seems, as foreign direct investment in Indonesia is not exclusively limited to the Chinese.[14]

Concluding Observations

Indonesia is now dealing with the challenges posed by other countries' approaches and strategies toward the Indo-Pacific region. Indonesia's diplomacy towards China can be characterised by both geopolitical competition and geoeconomic cooperation. From 2013 to 2016, there were increasing conflicts and confrontations between China and Indonesia over the fishing areas in the Natuna Islands. These seas are where China's "9-dash line" claim overlaps with Indonesia's Exclusive Economic Zone (EEZ). The Chinese assertions were met with dismay by the Indonesian military (Moeldoko, 2014).

In May 2018, China and Indonesia released a Joint Statement acknowledging the progress made since establishing the China-Indonesia Comprehensive Strategic Partnership. They specifically highlighted the successful integration of China's 21st Century Maritime Silk Road initiative with Indonesia's Vision of Global Maritime Fulcrum. Moreover, projects including Jakarta-Bandung High-Speed Railway Project which is jointly developed under the Regional Comprehensive Economic Corridor within the Belt and Road Initiative cooperation and the Global Maritime Fulcrum framework along with the efforts to reach a conclusion on the Code of Conduct on the South China Sea. (Indonesia-China, 2018). [15]

Indonesia's emphasis on ASEAN as a persistent regional platform reflects traditional regionalism. However, the challenge with applying traditional regionalism lies in the lack of a well-structured Indo-Pacific region. The closest attempt at structuring is the East Asia Summit (EAS). However, it has limited ability to integrate due to conflicting visions for the Indo-Pacific by India, Indonesia, China, Japan, and the United States highlighting the advent of regionalism and geopolitics. Indonesia has faced challenges in gaining support from the EAS for its Indo-Pacific ideas due to the conflicting perspectives on the concept of region. Additionally, there is growing apprehension about China's increasing naval presence in the Western Pacific and the Indian Ocean and its Western criticism of "debt diplomacy" through the Maritime Silk Road.

There is a risk that Indonesia's Indo-Pacific outlook may be impacted greatly due to its unresolved naval deficiencies, growing pressure from major powers, a split and weak ASEAN, unenforceable norms, and a weakly defined and less than effective multilateral approach. An Indonesian commentator expressed a straightforward view, stating that Indonesia's Indo-Pacific perspective is based rather on the limited options available; he also suggests that Indonesia's primary objective is to avoid getting involved in conflicts (Sulaiman, 2019)

The Indonesian development cooperation activities can be comprehended through South-South collaboration. In 1946, Indonesia dispatched over 500,000 tons of rice to India at the time when India was experiencing a severe famine. The provision of early humanitarian aid contributed to the country's acknowledgment by its southern counterparts and reinforced its standing on the international stage.[16] Indonesia, as the founder of the Non-Aligned Movement (NAM), is recognized for fostering technical cooperation among developing nations in fields like agriculture, fisheries, and family planning. In 1995, Indonesia established the NAM Centre for South-South Technical Cooperation, aimed to tackle poverty, support the growth of small and medium enterprises (SMEs), promote agricultural development, improve healthcare, safeguard the environment, and advance information and communication technologies. Additionally, Indonesia has long practiced triangular cooperation by partnering with a developed country and multilateral organisations. This approach has allowed Indonesia to actively contribute to knowledge transfer, capacity building, and expertise sharing initiatives. Between 2000 and 2013, Indonesia allocated approximately US$ 49.8 million toward South-South and triangular cooperation efforts. Extending this model to the Indo-Pacific region, Indonesia reaffirmed its commitment to Pacific Island Countries (PICs) through the 'Bali Message for Development Cooperation', which was announced at the Indonesia-Pacific Forum for Development in December 2022.

Moreover, according to the World Bank report (2024), Indonesia's economy is projected to see an average annual growth rate of 5.1% from 2024 to 2026. These problems include declining commodity boom, growing geopolitical uncertainty and heightened volatility in food and energy prices.[17] Interestingly, the 43rd ASEAN Summit held significant importance for Indonesia as it presented a complex network of favourable circumstances and potential risks. The summit served as a crucial test for Indonesia's capacity to guide ASEAN towards stability and coherence among the complex challenges of internal conflicts and external influences. As Indonesia assumed the chairmanship, it had a chance to recalibrate the course for itself and the broader ASEAN region. This critical moment could shape the bloc's future direction for a long time and demonstrate whether Indonesia is only an observer in the area or a catalyst for significant change.[18]

However, successfully addressing the challenge in 2024 and beyond would necessitate maintaining these different focus areas and implementing more extensive initiatives. The convergence of many crises highlights the necessity for all member states to embrace a broader understanding of their national interests. Developing the post-2025 vision for the ASEAN Community also provides a chance to analyse institutional processes that could enhance the responsiveness and adaptability of ASEAN. Member nations must consistently implement steps to protect themselves from escalating major power rivalry, influence the broader context, and even surpass it through skilful balancing and involvement. This will enhance Southeast Asia's autonomy and accelerate its economic development rather than relegating the area to a subordinate position under the dominant global powers. [19] Finally, it goes without saying that India would continue to support both ASEAN and Indonesia in their efforts to achieve peace, stability and prosperity in the region.

NOTES

1 https://www.orfonline.org/expert-speak/indias-growing-strategic-footprint-in-the-indo-pacific
2 https://www.jointproject.eu/wp-content/uploads/2023/02/joint_rp_14.pdf
3 https://foreignpolicy.com/2021/08/26/indonesia-china-us-geopolitics/
4 https://www.asean.emb-japan.go.jp/files/000352880.pdf
5 https://foreignpolicy.com/2021/08/26/indonesia-china-us-geopolitics/
6 https://eastasiaforum.org/2023/12/09/keeping-the-ipef-afloat-is-in-indonesias-interest/
7 https://www.thejakartapost.com/news/2018/12/19/china-welcomes-asean-s-indo-pacific.html
8 US Mission to ASEAN. (2019, July 2). The United States welcomes the 'ASEAN Outlook on the Indo-Pacific' [Press statement]. Retrieved from https://asean.usmission.gov/the-united-states-welcomes-the-aseanoutlook- on-the-indo-pacific/.
9 https://blogs.worldbank.org/en/trade/indonesia-can-use-trade-policies-to-accelerate-its-green-transfo#:~:text=While%20Indonesia%20has%20committed%20to,of%20these%20is%20strongly%20enforceabe
10 https://www.trade.gov/country-commercial-guides/indonesia-trade-agreements
11 https://asean2023.id/en/news/indonesias-important-involvement-in-asean-issues
12 https://www.ris.org.in/sites/default/files/Publication/1-India%20Indonesia%20 Panel %20 Discussion%20Report.pdf
13 https://www.ris.org.in/sites/default/files/Publication/1-India%20Indonesia%20 Panel %20 Discussion%20Report.pdf
14 Ibid.
15 Indonesia-China (2018) Full text of China-Indonesia joint statement, 8 May. Available at: http://www.xinhuanet.com/english/2018-05/08/c_137163660.html
16 https://www.orfonline.org/research/navigating-the-indo-pacific-development-cooperation-as-a-diplomatic-tool#_edn62
17 https://www.worldbank.org/en/news/press-release/2024/06/24/indonesia-economy-projected-to-remain-resilient#:~:text=Indonesia's%20gross%20domestic%20product%20growth, prices%2C %20and%20rising%20geopolitical%20uncertainty.
18 https://thediplomat.com/2023/09/indonesias-asean-chairmanship-could-make-or-break-the-bloc/
19 https://www.9dashline.com/article/in-forum-2024-the-future-of-asean

REFERENCES

1. Agastia G and Perwita A (2015) Jokowi's maritime axis: change and continuity of Indonesia's role in Indo-Pacific. Journal of ASEAN Studies 3(1): 32-41.
2. Agastia, I. G. B. D. (2020). Understanding Indonesia's role in the 'ASEAN Outlook on the Indo Pacific': A role theory approach. *Asia & the Pacific Policy Studies, 7*(3), 293-305.
3. Anwar, D. F. (2020). Indonesia and the ASEAN outlook on the Indo-Pacific. *International Affairs, 96*(1),111-129. https://doi.org/10.1093/ia/iiz223
4. Anya, A. (2018). China welcomes ASEAN's Indo-Pacific. Retrieved from https://www.thejakartapost.com/news/2018/12/19/china-welcomes-asean-s-indo-pacific.html
5. Aufiya MA (2017) Indonesia's global maritime fulcrum: Contribution in the Indo-Pacific region. *Journal of International Studies* 6(2): 143–159.
6. Hill, Hal and Deasy Pane. 2018. 'Indonesia and the Global Economy: Missed Opportunities?' In *Indonesia in the New World: Globalisation, Nationalism and Sovereignty*. Edited by Arianto A. Patunru, Mari Pangestu, and M. Chatib Basri, 267–93. Singapore: ISEAS Publishing.

7. Moeldoko G (2014) China's dismaying new claims in the South China Sea. Wall Street Journal, 24 April. Available at: https://www.wsj.com/articles/moeldoko-chinas-dismaying-new-claims-inthe- south-china-sea-1398382003 (accessed 7 March 2019).
8. Pane, Deasy and Arianto A. Patunru. 2023. 'The Role of Imported Inputs in Firms' Productivity and Exports: Evidence from Indonesia'. *Review of World Economics* 159: 629–72. doi: 10.1007/s10290-022-00476-z
9. Pangestu, Mari, Sjamsu Rahardja and Lili Yan Ing. 2015. 'Fifty Years of Trade Policy in Indonesia: New World Trade, Old Treatments'. *Bulletin of Indonesian Economic Studies* 51 (2): 239–61. doi: 10.1080/00074918.2015.1061915.
10. Patunru, Arianto A. and Tarsidin. 2012. 'Recent Indonesian Economic Development and the Urgent Need to Remove Key Growth Obstacles'. *Asian Economic Papers* 11 (3): 57–77. doi: 10.1162/ASEP_a_00164
11. Patunru, Arianto A., Mari Pangestu and M. Chatib Basri, eds. 2018. *Indonesia in the New World: Globalisation, Nationalism and Sovereignty*. Singapore: ISEAS Publishing.
12. Scott, D. (2019). Indonesia grapples with the Indo-Pacific: Outreach, strategic discourse, and diplomacy. *Journal of Current Southeast Asian Affairs, 38*(2), 194-217.
13. Sulaiman Y (2019) Whither Indonesia's "Indo-Pacific Strategy"? Asie Visions (Afri), No. 105, Ifri, January.
14. Weatherbee, D. (2019). Indonesia, ASEAN, and the Indo-Pacific Cooperation Concept. *ISEAS Perspective* No. 47. Retrieved from http://hdl.handle.net/11540/10354.

Index

5G, 121

Abdurrahman Wahid (Gusdur), 27
Aceh-Andaman Connectivity Initiative, 7
Adani Power, 72
Affandi, 23
Afghanistan, 34
Africa, 8
Afro-Asian Solidarity, 92
American Century, 18
American Civil Rights Movement, 2
Amravati Buddha, 47
Andaman & Nicobar Islands, 35, 93
Andaman Sea, 7
Antony, A.K., 84
Apollo Hospitals, 4
Aramane, Giridhar, 85
Archipelagic Sea Lanes (ALKI), 80
Archipelago, 36
Arjuna-Vivaha, 38
Artificial Intelligence (AI), 73, 76
ASEAN Cultural Heritage List, 122
ASEAN Defence Ministers' Meeting Plus (ADMM-Plus), 94, 102
ASEAN Economic Ministers-India Consultations (AEM+India), 116, 120
ASEAN Inter-Parliamentary Assembly (AIPA), 117
ASEAN Outlook on the Indo-Pacific (AOIP), 120, 126
ASEAN Plus Three (APT), 28
ASEAN Regional Forum (ARF), 26, 31, 94, 102, 105, 116
ASEAN-India Artists' Camp, 121
ASEAN-India Business Council (AIBC), 120
ASEAN-India Comprehensive Strategic Partnership (CSP), 116
ASEAN-India Cooperation Fund (AIF), 116
ASEAN-India Foreign Ministers Meeting (AIFMM), 116
ASEAN-India Green Fund (AIGF), 116
ASEAN-India Joint Cooperation Committee (AIJCC), 116
ASEAN-India, 6, 75
  Joint Statement on Maritime Cooperation, 119
  Maritime Exercise, 117, 125
  Media Exchange Visits, 121
  Music Festival, 121
  Network of Universities, 122
  Start-up Festival, 121
  Youth Summit, 121
ASEAN-India Ministerial Meeting on Agriculture and Forestry (AIMMAF), 116
ASEAN-India Science and Technology Development Fund (AISTDF), 116
ASEAN-India Senior Officials Meeting (AISOM), 116
ASEAN-India Trade in Goods Agreement (AITIGA), 5, 8, 32, 120
ASEAN-India Working Group on Science and Technology (AIWGST), 116
Asia Pacific Economic Cooperation, 26
Asia-Africa Conference, 1, 15
Asia-Africa Growth Corridor (AAGC), 102
Asian Relations Conference, 3, 22, 39, 92
Assam, 46
Association of South East Asian Nations (ASEAN), 12, 25, 27-31, 35-36, 42, 91-92, 101-02, 108, 117, 119, 121, 125-26, 130, 132-33

Australia, 28, 99-100, 126, 129

Bahasa, 38, 48
Bali, 7-8
Bali Declaration, 5
Bali Jatra, 92
Balinese Ramakavaca, 56
Bandung Afro-Asian Conference, 23
Bandung Conference, 1, 3, 9, 15-16
Bandung 2.0, 7, 9
Bangladesh, 34
Bank Indonesia (BI), 75
Barong Temple, 51
Bastian, Adolf, 36
Bay of Bengal, 7, 93
Bay of Bengal Initiative for Multi-Sector Technical and Economic Cooperation (BIMSTEC) , 7, 8, 34-35
Bharat-yuddha, 38
Bhattara, 38
Bhinneka Tunggal Ika, 4
Bhutan, 34
Biennial Defence Ministers' Forum, 84
Blue Economy, 97, 119
Bogor Conference, 23
Bollywood Bali, 79
Bonhomie, Bandung, 2-3
Borobudur Stupa, 55
Borobudur Temple, 12, 51, 54, 58, 92
Brahma, 51
Brahmanda Purana, 38
Brazil, 18
BRICS, 6, 32
British Century, 18
Brunei, 46
Brunei Darussalam, 126
Buddhism, 12, 45, 49-51, 54
Buddhist, 37, 54
Burma, 1, 15, 23, 46

Cambodia, 36, 93, 130
Candi Ijo, 51
Central Java, 50, 54
Ceylon, 1, 23
Chakravartin, 50
Chile, 129
China, 1-2, 13, 16-18, 23, 28-30, 32, 45, 96, 102, 118, 126, 131-32
China's "9-dash line", 131
China's Belt and Road Initiative (BRI), 100
Chinese
  Century, 18
  Dream, 18
Climate Change, 97
Coalition of Disaster Resilient Infrastructure (CDRI), 6
Coedes, George, 37
Cold War, 2, 16, 19, 25-26, 92, 118
Colombo Powers, 15, 23, 25
Common Era, 37, 48
Computer Emergency Response Teams (CERTs), 107
Confidence-Building Measures (CBMs), 83, 85, 88
COP 21, 6
Cottey and Foster, 83
COVID-19, 31, 39
Cyber Threat Hunting Webinar, 121
Cybersecurity, 105
Cybersecurity Capacity-Building, 112

Dasa Sila, 1, 3
Defence Capabilities, 83
Defence Cooperation Agreement, 40, 81
Defence Diplomacy Activities, 82-83
Defence Industry Development, 84
Defense White Paper, 81
Delhi Declaration, 5
Delhi Dialogue, 117
Delhi-Jakarta, 91
Devi Mahishasurmardini, 47
Dieng Plateau, 55, 57, 58
Digital Technology, 131
Disaster Risk Management, 97
Distant Water Fishing (DWF), 41
Double Taxation Avoidance Agreement, 73
Dr Krom, 46

East Asia, 18
East Asia Summit (EAS), 21, 28, 30-31, 93, 102, 116, 132
East Borneo (Kalimantan), 52
East Indies, 36
East Java, 55
East Kalimantan (Borneo), 48
Eastern Bengal, 46
Economic Cooperation, 96
Egypt, 1, 2
Electric Vehicle (EV), 75-76, 128
Environmental Protection, 97
EU, 8
Exclusive Economic Zone (EEZ), 29
Expanded ASEAN Maritime Forum, 116
Extended Neighbourhood, 35

Far East, 80
Farther India, 36
Fiji, 126
Five-Point Consensus (5PC), 130
France, 6
Free and Open Indo-Pacific Strategy, 125
Free Trade Agreements (FTAs), 8, 129
Further India, 36

G15, 25
G20, 5-8, 12, 21, 30-32, 42, 71, 91-92
Gandhi, Indira, 24-25
Gandhi, Rajiv, 25
Garuda Purana, 38
GDP, 12, 14
General Wiranto, 27
Ghana, 1
Global Biofuel Alliance (GBA), 6
Global Cyber Security Cooperation Portal, 109
Global Cybersecurity Index (GCI), 106, 111
Global Forum on Cyber Expertise, 108
Global Maritime Fulcrum (GMF), 80, 118
Global South, 1, 2, 8, 12, 91, 112
Gold Coast, 1
Greater India, 36
Gunavarman, 50

Hansen, Peo, 2
Harbour Phase, 87
Harivamsha, 38
Hinduism, 12, 49-51, 54
Horta, José Ramos, 8
Humanitarian Assistance and Disaster Relief (HADR), 7, 94-95, 100-01, 120

Iceland, 129
Illegal, Unreported and Unregulated (IUU) Fishing, 7, 82, 95
India, 1, 3, 5-9, 13-15, 17-18, 21-22, 24-25, 28-29, 32, 35, 40, 45, 81, 84, 91-92, 97-100, 112, 121-22, 124, 126, 128, 132
India Indonesia Energy Forum, 72
India's Act East Policy, 30, 93, 101-02, 119
India's Kilo Class Submarine, 125
India's Look East Policy, 93, 118, 130
India-ASEAN Free Trade Area (FTA), 73
India-ASEAN Relations, 6, 28, 115-16
India-Brazil-South Africa Dialogue Forum, 6
India-China Dynamics, 3
India-France Ties, 6
India-Indonesia, 79
    Economic and Financial Dialogue, 31, 75
    Relations, 118
India-Indonesia Bilateral Investment Treaty (BIT), 74
India-Indonesia Comprehensive Economic Partnership Agreement (CEPA), 73
India-Indonesia Coordinated Patrol (Ind-Indo Corpat), 86-88, 102
India-Indonesia Security Dialogue (IISD), 86, 88
India-Indonesia-Australia Framework, 7
India-Malaysia-Thailand Growth Triangle, 7
Indian Archipelago, 36
Indian Investments in Indonesia, 74
Indian Maritime Security Strategy, 41
Indian Navy, 29, 39, 41
Indian Navy's Information Fusion Centre for the Indian Ocean Region (IFC-IOR), 100
Indian Ocean Marine Resources, 97
Indian Ocean Naval Symposium (IONS), 102

Indian Ocean Region (IOR), 41, 126
Indian Ocean Rim Association (IORA), 6, 12, 29, 75, 91-95, 97, 98, 102, 118, 126
  Fisheries Support Unit and Working Group on Blue Economy, 97
  Maritime Safety and Security Working Group, 96
Indian Ocean, 10, 80-82, 93-94, 96, 98-99
Indian Ocean Zone of Peace, 118
India-Pakistan Conflict, 24
Indonesia, 1, 5-9, 14-15, 17, 21-22, 24, 29, 32, 35-36, 40, 42, 46, 48, 56-57, 80-81, 84, 87, 91-93, 97-100, 112, 119, 122, 124-28, 130-32
  Conference on , 92
Indonesia Africa Forum (IAF), 8
Indonesia Emas (Golden Indonesia), 4
Indonesia's
  Aceh, 93
  Exclusive Economic Zone (EEZ), 131
  Exports to India, 62
  Global Maritime Fulcrum Policy, 82, 102
  Investment in India, 74
Indonesia's National Agency for Disaster Management (BNPB), 98
Indo-Pacific Economic Framework for Prosperity (IPEF), 126-27
Indo-Pacific Oceans Initiative (IPOI), 30, 95
Indo-Pacific Treaty of Friendship and Cooperation (IPTFC), 125
Indo-Pacific, 42, 80-81, 87, 101
INS Delhi, 23, 125
INS Sindhu Kesari, 125
International Big Cat Alliance (IBCA), 6
International Conference on ASEAN India Cultural and Civilisational Links, 122
International Solar Alliance (ISA), 6
International Telecommunication Union's (ITU), 106, 111
Internet of Things (IoT), 73, 121
Islamabad, 34
Islands of India, 36
IT, 76, 79

Jaishankar, Dr S., 35
Jakarta, 21, 77, 81, 87
Jakarta East Asia Summit, 6
Jakarta-Bandung High-Speed Railway Project, 72, 131
Jammu and Kashmir, 40
Japan, 17-18, 22, 28, 126, 132
Jataka, 38
Java (Yavadvipa), 11, 21, 45, 50, 55, 77
Joint Commission Meeting (JCM), 75
Joint Defence Cooperation Committee (JDCC), 84-85, 88
Joint Working Group, 85
Joko Widodo (Jokowi), 8, 29-30, 80, 95
Jonsson, Stefan, 2

Kakawin Ramayana, 56
Kalasan, 54
Kalla, Jusuf, 30
Kartika, 23
Katha-Sarit Sagara, 38
Kawi, 38
Kazan, 6
King Mulavarman, 52
King Purnawarman, 52, 53
King Vadhaka, 50
Korean Peninsula, 17, 28, 126
Krom, Dr N. J., 11, 45
Kshemendra's Ramayana-Manjari, 38
Kulhudhuffushi, 35
Kutai Martadipura Kingdom, 52
Kutai, 48

L&T, 72
Lakshadweep Islands, 35
Land of Gold, 36
Lee Kuan Yew, 29
Liechtenstein, 129
Local Currency Settlement System (LCSS), 5
Lord Buddha, 47
Lord Shiva, 51, 54
Lord Vishnu, 47, 51

Maddison, 13

Maddison, Angus, 12
Madhyadesa, 53
Mahabharata, 55
Mahaniddesa, 46
Maharajah, 50
Maharajahs of Srivijaya, 50
Mahayana Buddhism, 54
Mahindra & Mahindra, 72
Majapahit, 37
Malacca Straits Patrol (MSP), 7
Malacca Straits, 94
Malay Peninsula, 46
Malaysia, 24, 40, 46, 124, 126
Maldives, 35
Manipur, 46
Maritime
  Diplomacy, 17
  Safety and Security, 119
  Security Cooperation, 82, 95
Maritime Domain Awareness (MDA), 100
Markandeya Purana, 38
Marsudi, Retno, 40
Masala Bumbu, 21-22
Mataram Dynasty, 51
Mataram Kingdom, 54
Matsya Purana, 38
Mayapada Hospitals, 4
Memorandum of Understanding (MoU), 28-29, 75, 81
Mendut, 54
Micro, Small, and Medium Enterprises (MSMEs), 131
Middle East, 17
MILAN, 118
Milinda-panha, 38
Milindapanha, 46
MIT Cyber Defense Index, 106
Modern Indonesia, 30
Modi, Narendra, 6, 29-30, 34-36, 41, 81, 93
Modi-Widodo Summit, 81
Moro National Liberation Front (MNLF), 130
Mosaics of Cultures, 92
Mozambique, 129
Muara Jambi, 21
Muhammadiyah, 30
Myanmar, 93, 130
  Rohingya Issue in, 31

Nalanda, 21
National Cybersecurity Index (NCSI), 106
National Disaster Management Authority (NDMA), 98
NatStrat, 5
Natuna Besar, 41
Natuna Sea, 29
Natural Disasters, 98
Navy-to-Navy Talks (NTNT), 85, 88
Nehru, Jawaharlal, 16, 23-24, 39, 92
Nehru-Sukarno, 22
Neighbourhood First, 34
New Delhi, 6, 21, 34, 39, 85
New Order Government, 25
New Order Period, 24, 26-27
New York, 17
New Zealand, 28, 126
Niddesa, 38
Non-Aligned Movement (NAM), 3, 15-16, 21, 23, 26, 92, 118, 132
  Centre for South-South Technical Cooperation, 132
Norway, 129
Nusantara, 36
Nustantara (IKN), 4

Odisha, 92
Old Javanese, 38
Open-Ended Working Group, 108-09
Operation Crow, 3
Operation Gambhir, 39
Operation Samudra Setu, 39
Organisation of Islamic Cooperation, 31, 40

Pacific Island Countries (PICs), 133
Pakistan, 1, 15, 23, 34
Palestine, 31
Pallawa, 11
Paris, 6

Patnaik, Biju, 22, 39
Peninsular Malaysia, 38
Periplus, 46
Piracy, 96
Plan of Action, 121
Plaosan, 54
Port of Palur, 46
post-Cold War world, 26
post-New Order era, 25
Prambanan, 12, 51, 54, 58
President Habibie, 27
Programme of Action (PoA), 110
Ptolemy, 46
Ptolemy, Geographical Hyphegesis, 11
Public-Private Partnerships (PPPs), 73

Quad, 7, 32, 120, 122

Ramayana, 21, 55-56
Reddy, N. Sanjeeva, 25
Regional Comprehensive Economic Corridor, 131
Regional Comprehensive Economic Partnership (RCEP), 120
Rekindling Bandung, 5
Research and Development (R&D), 121
Reserve Bank of India (RBI), 75
Revolusi, 2
Reybrouck, David Van, 2
Royal Enfield, 72
Russia, 18
Russia-China on Ukraine, 6
Ryacudu, General (Retd.) Ryamizard, 84

Sabang, 35
Sagar Mala, 95
Sage Agastya, 38
Samudra Shakti Exercise, 84, 87
San Francisco Conference, 1
Sanatan Dharma (Hinduism), 45
SAREX, 118
Satyameva Jayate, 4
Science and Technology, 119
Scott, 125
Sea Phase, 87
Security and Growth for All in the Region (SAGAR), 81-82
Sewu, 51, 54
SEZs, 4
Shailendra, 37
Shared Vision on Maritime Cooperation in the Indo-Pacific, 81
Shiva Linga, 47
Shivaite King Sanjaya, 51
Singapore, 8, 126
Singh, Dr Manmohan, 28
Sino-Indian Conflict, 24
Small and Medium Enterprises (SMEs), 132
Sojomerto Inscription, 54
Somalia, 96
South Asia, 35, 76
South Asian Association for Regional Cooperation (SAARC), 34, 42
South China Sea (SCS), 29, 41, 102, 118, 124-25
Southeast Asia, 14, 18, 36, 38, 40, 45, 46, 76, 93, 117
  Day, 92
Southernising, 2
South-South Cooperation, 8, 25, 132
Sri Lanka, 15
Srivijaya Empire, 53
Sri-Vijaya, 37
Standard International Trade Classification, 61
Stealth frigate INS Satpura, 125
Straits of Malacca, 41
Strategic Defense Review (UK Ministry of Defence), 82
Strategic Engagement, 83
Sukarno, 16, 22-23, 37
Sukarnoputri, Megawati, 27
Sumatra, 21
Sunda Straits, 87
Surabaya, 84
Susilo Bambang Yudhoyono (SBY), 27-28
Sustainable Development Goals (SDGs), 72
Sustainable Development of Marine Resources, 119

Suvarnabhumi, 36, 46
Suvarnadvipa, 38, 46
Switzerland, 129

Tablighi Jamaat, 31
Tarumanagara Kingdom, 52
Tata Motors, 72
Tata Power, 72
Tatang River, 54
Taufanto, Air Marshal Donny Ermawan, 85
Thailand, 7, 126
the Netherlands, 15
the Philippines, 124, 126, 130
Third World, 1
Trade and Investment, 119
Trilateral Dialogue on Indian Ocean (TDIO), 98-101, 118
Tsunami, 39
TVS, 72

Ulama, Nahdlatul, 30
UN Group of Governmental Experts
  on Developments in the Field of Information and Telecommunications in the Context of International Security, 107-08
UN Open-ended Working Group (OEWG), 109-10
Unified Payments Interface (UPI), 76
United Arab Emirates (UAE), 40
United Kingdom (UK), 8, 82
United Nations (UN), 1, 2, 109
United Nations Convention on the Law of the Sea (UNCLOS), 100
United Nations General Assembly, 107
United Nations Peacekeeping Force (UNPF), 40
United Nations Security Council (UNSC), 3, 8, 40
United States (US), 2, 13, 17-18, 24-25, 28, 30, 102, 124, 126-27, 132
  Free and Open Indo-Pacific Agenda, 127
USSR/Soviet Union, 3, 16, 24

Vajpayee, Atal Behari, 28
Valmiki's Ramayana, 38
Vamana Purana, 38
Vayu Purana, 38
Vietnam, 126
Vietnam War, 24-25
Vishnu Purana, 38
Voice of Global South Summits (VOGSS), 8
Vyala, 55

Wang Yi, 127
Washington Consensus, 18
Washington, 17
West, 6, 26
West Asia, 45
West Irian, 24
West Java, 52
West Pacific, 18
Western Europe, 12
Western Java, 11
World Bank, 61, 129, 133
World Integrated Trade Solution (WITS), 61
World War II, 21
Wright, Richard, Color Curtain, 2

Xi Jinping, 18

Yali, 55
Yava-dvipa (Java), 38
Yavadvipa, 47
Yijing, 53
Yogyakarta, 22
Yohannes Sulaiman, 7
Yupa Inscriptions, 51